The #1 Guide to Performance Appraisals

Doing It Right!

James E. Neal Jr.

Author of the five-star best-seller
Effective Phrases for Performance Appraisals

The #1 Guide to Performance Appraisals

Doing It Right!

Publishing since 1978

Neal Publications, Inc.
127 West Indiana Avenue
Perrysburg, Ohio 43551

Publishers of

Effective Phrases for Performance Appraisals
a guide to successful evaluations

Effective Resume Writing
a guide to successful employment

*Effective Letters for Business
Professional and Personal Use*
a guide to successful correspondence

Your Slice of the Melon
a guide to greater job success

The #1 Guide to Performance Appraisals

Doing It Right!

Neal Publications, Inc.
127 West Indiana Avenue
P.O. Box 451
Perrysburg, Ohio 43552-0451
USA

First Edition	2001
Second Printing	2001
Third Printing	2002

Copyright 2001 by
James E. Neal, Jr.
Printed in the United States of America

Library of Congress Control Number: 2001130060
ISBN 1-882423-46-1
SAN 240-8198

This publication is designed to provide accurate and authoritative information in regard to the subject matter covered. It is sold with the understanding that the publisher is not engaged in rendering legal, accounting, or other professional services. If legal advice or other expert assistance is required, the services of a competent professional person should be sought.

Be a member of the construction gang—
not the wrecking crew.

unknown

Contents

Foreword

This book is a practical, down-to-earth guide to performance appraisals. It is not intended to be a lengthy academic approach to the subject. You will not find chapters such as "What Is Work"?

I have a wealth of experience in developing and administering appraisal programs. My experience covers every phase of the subject, including wrongful discharge litigation.

My book entitled *Effective Phrases for Performance Appraisals* has undergone 57 printings and is now in its ninth edition. It has been a best-seller for many years and has been used extensively in seminars and training programs.

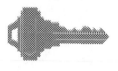 Major points in this book are highlighted by a key in the margin. The keys are summarized in the last chapter. This system permits evaluators to refresh themselves on key points prior to each rating period, without rereading the entire book.

This book is concisely written and is intended to be a valuable guide to all persons involved in the appraisal process. I hope that you will find it informative and helpful.

James E. Neal Jr.

Chapter I

◆

Trends and Developments

Perhaps no two words in organizational life instill more fear and trepidation than performance appraisals. Many persons consider appraisals to be in the same category as an Internal Revenue Service (IRS) audit.

Regardless of how you feel, performance reviews are in universal use everywhere. In fact, evaluations are spreading far beyond the work environment. Today, you are asked to rate restaurant service, quality of food, price, etc. If you buy a new car, you will receive many phone calls and survey forms. You will be asked questions regarding the sales person, vehicle operation, and service. Everyone from the CEO to the golf caddie is being evaluated.

The word *appraisal* comes from the Latin word *"appratiare"* meaning to set a price or value. In effect, employees trade work for compensation, and management decides the degree of both values and compensation.

In writing this book, a number of old business books were consulted dating back to the late 1890s. If you look in the old books under "P" for performance, you will find only "penmanship." It is not until the early 1950s when you begin to see coverage of performance appraisals in the business literature. Apparently, few organizations had formal evaluation programs in the first half of the Twentieth Century; performance and compensation were based strictly on seniority and feelings. Many employers simply gave across-the-board increases with little attention given to "pay for performance."

The concept of pay for performance was an outgrowth of recession years when companies found it necessary to trim costs and increase efficiency for prolonged recovery. Formal appraisals gained widespread support in the '80s, largely due to the need for an equitable means of determining pay increases. Today, performance evaluations are widespread and sophisticated.

Performance appraisals are now being conducted in a work environment far different from years ago. Employees no longer can count on a career with a single employer. Workers are less loyal and place greater emphasis on individualism and identify less with the organization. Higher levels of education and a spirit of entrepreneurship have led many employees to view themselves more as independent contractors than employees.

Employers have also changed their employment policies. Flexible work scheduling, work at home, casual attire, exercise facilities, and the offering of a wide range of investment plans have all affected employee attitudes.

As a result of surging technology in the workplace, more and more employers are closely monitoring the activities of employees. Many employers, especially in large firms, are continuously monitoring e-mail, Internet usage, computer files, and even listening in on telephone conversations. Workplace surveillance is being used for purposes of policy conformance, output measurements, performance evaluations, and legal concerns. Employee behavior is being scrutinized as never before with the full protection of court rulings.

Employees want to be measured against objective standards that are mutually understood and communicated. If employees are recognized and rewarded for superior performance, they are more likely to continue at a high level of achievement.

Employees want to know how well they are doing and appreciate feedback. Persons who are performing well want to be recognized by the boss.

If not properly handled, performance appraisals can create resentment and resistance among employees rather than improve performance.

Employees often believe that reviews are a waste of time and meaningless. Some management consultants and psychologists are critical of reviews because they are inconsistent and leave employees disenchanted.

Employers, however, argue that performance appraisals provide the only fair means of administering compensation and development programs. From an organizational viewpoint, performance appraisals are needed to achieve the following objectives:

- To identify the strengths and weaknesses of employees
- To identify the growth potential of employees
- To provide information for employee development
- To make the organization more productive
- To provide data for the fair compensation of employees
- To protect the organization from employment lawsuits

The compensation objective is certainly valid. How would you like to work for a company that based wage and salary increases on the style of your hair, the make of your car, or the neighborhood where you reside?

Managements may spend a tremendous amount of time and money developing effective evaluation programs. Meetings are often held to stress the benefits of sound appraisal skills such as career development and assessments for promotion.

Companies traditionally emphasize that appraisals are necessary to evaluate skills, measure performance, and plan for improvements. Special efforts are taken to make salary decisions at different times of the year to divorce them from performance review periods. Despite the best efforts of management, most employees recognize that their actual pay increase is the true measure of what the organization thinks of them.

Inherent Conflicts of Appraisals

The employee in every appraisal interview wishes to receive the highest rating in hopes of getting a sizable pay increase. Managers, however, are often operating under strict budget restraints and wish to keep everyone reasonably satisfied. The appraiser is often under strong pressure to rate everyone as average in order to equally distribute the departmental budget.

With the large number of lawsuits claiming discriminatory discharges, it is understandable why employers need to take protective measures. Managers must now recognize that all of their ratings must be defensible in court.

Consultants Love Appraisals

To consultants, appraisals are a gold mine. Most consultants will tell you that only out-of-town experts can properly design an effective evaluation program. They believe that they are better qualified than in-house people who have an intricate knowledge of the organization. Management often takes a favorable view of consultants because it is easier to introduce a program prepared by an outsider who can then be blamed for any unfavorable results.

New Corporate Structures and the Appraisal Merry-Go-Round

The high number of corporate acquisitions, mergers, and restructures in recent years has resulted in new appraisal programs for many employees. The parent company often wishes to have a standard program in place for all its companies and divisions. Computerization has provided a major thrust for company-wide evaluation programs. Today, many long-term employees have been evaluated under a parade of different programs.

Impact of Human Resources

Human Resources (HR) departments often have an image problem. They are too frequently looked upon as a necessary but not a core and profit-producing contributor. The effectiveness of an appraisal program may very well depend on the relative influence and management support of the HR function in a particular organization.

To some HR personnel, appraisals mean endless meetings, and continuous revisions of forms, graphs, charts, and reports. Whenever things are slow, there are always appraisal forms to tinker with. As soon as a new human resources director arrives on the scene, you can usually be sure that new appraisal forms and procedures will soon follow.

Many companies are in a continuous state of revising appraisal programs because the last one didn't work. A downside of continuous revisions is that it makes it extremely difficult to track the performance of long-term employees. Sound evaluation programs remain in place for a period of time and are only revised to meet changes in working conditions.

Key areas of HR concern tend to occur in cycles. A review of archives of appraisal forms over the past two decades reveal the following cycles of special interest:

1. assertiveness

2. quality

3. empowerment

4. team building

5. legal

What sometimes happens is that HR managers strive to keep their companies on the cutting edge. If books, articles, and seminars emphasize team building, then your appraisal forms are changed to stress this new interest. An aggressive HR executive will convince top management of the need to fully support the latest fad. Within a short period of time, the company's annual report will highlight participation in this dramatic new development. A year or two later, emphasis on this management breakthrough often disappears.

Growing Difficulties of Appraisals

In many respects, performance appraisals are becoming more difficult because of the following:

- Downsizing in middle management is requiring more evaluations per manager.

- Computers are decreasing personal contact.

- More persons are working for multiple superiors.

- The increasing mobility among evaluators and employees is weakening the continuity.

• Legal concerns require more valid and objective measurement standards that must be defensible.

It's easy to evaluate personnel with clearly definable standards of measurement such as percent of sales objective achieved or the percent of defects. The task becomes much more difficult when evaluating administrative personnel where measurements must be more subjective.

You need to recognize that it takes the varied talents of many people to make a corporation run smoothly. A scientist may have a brilliant mind but not the outgoing personality of a dynamic sales manager. Both types of personalities play an important role in orchestrating the success of the organization.

Performance Appraisals Are Much More Than a Form

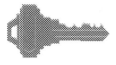

Appraisal forms must be clearly developed to meet the requirements of specific positions or groups of positions. Using the same form to evaluate personnel in completely different areas of the company is unrealistic.

Appraisals must be viewed in a much larger context than a detailed form. Appraisal forms are only one segment of a large program designed to make the organization more productive and successful.

A common misbelief is that a well-designed form will result in a perfect evaluation program. The truth is that an effective system is based on a frank, honest, and straightforward discussion between manager and employee involving expectations, how well the job is being performed, and plans for improvement and follow-up.

Considering the Costs

A considerable cost is involved in developing and maintaining a well-functioning appraisal system. Endless meetings and executive time must be devoted to:

- Conducting job analyses

- Developing job descriptions

- Designing forms

- Obtaining legal approval

- Training evaluators

- Scoring the forms

- Conducting interviews

- Implementing follow-up

- Storing the forms

- Assigning compensation values

- Developing succession and promotion plans

- Continuous monitoring and updating

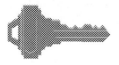

In a large corporation, interviews alone can consume hundreds or perhaps thousands of hours. Clearly, an effective program requires a total commitment from top management in both time and money.

Using Appraisals as a Recruiting Tool

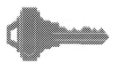

A very positive use of appraisals can be made in recruiting new employees. The interviewer can make the point that the company strives to develop every employee to their fullest potential. Recruiters can emphasize that evaluations are used continuously to take an inventory of the company's human talent. The point can be made that employees are also asked about their shortcomings, strengths, and long-term career goals. Prospective employees may be told that managers are required to know the talents and ambitions of their employees to ensure that they are able to promote worthy candidates whenever opportunities arise.

 Applicants appreciate knowing that the performance of all employees is formally reviewed at least once a year and at shorter intervals for new employees. The key in recruiting is to emphasize that good performance is fully recognized by the company.

Introducing a New Program

The introduction of a new evaluation program requires a sound and professional approach. After the whistles, sirens, and balloons, appraisals are too often viewed as more paperwork that needs to be filled out and periodically returned to HR.

It is critical that a new program be introduced by a top executive either in person, video, or in a written message. The introduction should emphasize that the new program is designed to help the organization better achieve its mission statement. Employees need to be assured that the program has the full backing of top management and is not the product of a self-serving executive looking for recognition.

Performance appraisals are one of the most perplexing issues in organizational life.

Chapter II

◆

Defining Job Descriptions

In large organizations, it is virtually impossible to establish a universal evaluation program based on common measurement standards that will cover manufacturing, research, finance, sales, and technical personnel. Job descriptions and measurement standards vary widely. A standard appraisal form used to rate secretaries is certainly not applicable to research scientists.

However, some characteristics do apply to everyone. Surely, you can rate both a secretary and a research scientist in such areas as knowledge of job, motivation, and communication skills. A well-designed evaluation program obviously must be developed to meet the specific needs of personnel in different fields.

The professional literature always emphasizes that evaluation forms need to be developed to meet specific responsibilities and measurement standards as outlined in job descriptions. This is easier said than done.

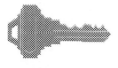 A large corporation may have hundreds of job descriptions. It obviously would be unrealistic to develop a specific evaluation form for each position. Therefore, you want

to develop forms that are reasonably applicable to general categories of positions such as:

- Management
- Administrative
- Clerical
- Technical
- Sales

Who Needs a Job Description?

Every person from the CEO to the mail room clerk requires a job description. How can one be evaluated and know what is expected without a job description?

Some companies devote more time to office layouts than to job descriptions. Hundreds of hours are spent pouring over blueprints, carpeting, etc. Yet, little attention is given to the jobs of the people who will fill those offices.

 The first step in developing an evaluation program is to have a job description properly prepared for every employee. A job analysis, preferably developed by a specialist, is required. It's not smart to have employees prepare their final job analysis; they may not be the most objective. However, it is valuable to learn of the employee's perception of the job by requiring completion of a form similar to the following:

Job Analysis Questionnaire
(to be completed by employee)

Job Title: _____

Department: _____

Employee's
Name: _____

Immediate
Supervisor's
Name and Title: _____

Describe the purpose of this Job:

_____

_____

_____

Describe the duties of this job in detail and in descending order of importance. Use additional sheets if required. Attach a copy of all forms used.

Approx. % of Time	Daily Duties

In addition to a listing of daily duties, employees are commonly asked to also provide the following:

Knowledge
>   What essential knowledge is needed to successfully perform in the job (for example, knowledge of machinery, suppliers, safety requirements, etc.)?

Skills
>   What are the essential skills needed to successfully perform in this job (for example, decision-making, delegating, and problem-solving)?

Traits
>   What are the essential traits needed to successfully perform in this job (for example, initiative, resourcefulness, and versatility)?

The job analysis will provide much of the information needed to prepare the job description. A sound job description will outline the following:

•   Basic responsibilities

•   Specific duties

•   Authorities

•   Reporting relationship

•   Standards of performance

General responsibilities and duties applicable to five major categories of job descriptions are as follows:

1. *Management*
    A. Develop and adhere to a mission statement.

    B. Establish organizational goals and objectives.

    C. Develop sound policies, strategies, and action plans to meet organizational goals and objectives.

    D. Exercise sound cost-control measures to ensure the financial soundness of the organization.

E. Ensure the continuous flow of quality products or services.

F. Provide an organizational structure for achieving maximum productivity and effectiveness.

G. Make full and effective use of all organizational resources.

H. Develop programs to maximize organizational productivity.

I. Ensure measures to improve and strengthen the abilities, talents, and contributions of all employees.

J. Ensure the development and proper administration of a performance evaluation program for all employees.

K. Promote harmony and a spirit of cooperation with all affiliated companies, divisions, and departments.

L. Keep informed of emerging trends and developments affecting the organization including competition, environmental, legal, governmental, and technological concerns.

M. Ensure the development and timely release of all reports needed to meet internal and external requirements.

N. Communicate effectively with the board of directors, shareholders, and employees.

O. Represent the organization in dealing with the public, government, investment analysts, and employees.

2. *Administrative*

A. Develop sound administrative methods and procedures.

B. Maintain and ensure accuracy of all administrative functions.

    C. Develop and administer effective cost-control programs.

    D. Develop and conform to approved budget requirements.

    E. Prepare in a timely manner all required reports, studies, and projects.

    F. Coordinate administrative functions with other relevant departments and work areas.

    G. Communicate fully and appropriately with customers and suppliers.

    H. Make efficient use of all equipment and materials.

    I. Evaluate effectively the performance of all employees.

    J. Ensure the continuous development of employees.

    K. Keep abreast of new technologies to improve administrative efficiency.

    L. Conduct special projects and assignments as requested.

3. *Clerical*

    A. Provide optimal and effective clerical support.

    B. Prepare letters, memos, reports, and other communications in a timely and professional manner.

    C. Maintain a sound filing system for fast and easy retrieval.

    D. Maintain accurate records with a minimum of duplication.

    E. Demonstrate effective telephone techniques.

    F. Make efficient use of all office equipment.

    G. Keep well-informed and proficient in computer uses and applications.

4. *Technical*

   A. Provide sound technical assistance to all departments, customers, and suppliers.

   B. Keep management informed of technical trends and developments.

   C. Conduct product quality and performance tests.

   D. Recommend technical improvements in products or services.

   E. Provide technical training to employees and customers.

   F. Communicate highly technical information in easily understood terms.

   G. Prepare technical manuals, catalogs, and training aids.

5. *Sales*

   A. Achieve or exceed sales quotas.

   B. Keep well-informed of product features and benefits.

   C. Demonstrate and maintain strong selling skills.

   D. Make effective sales presentations.

   E. Maintain a close knowledge of customer requirements.

   F. Develop and follow efficient and productive call patterns.

   G. Give appropriate attention to all levels and sizes of accounts.

   H. Develop new accounts.

   I. Follow-up on all customer problems.

   J. Make effective use of advertising, merchandising, selling aids, marketing research, and technical support programs.

K. Maintain in proper condition all company-owned and leased equipment.

L. Demonstrate sound judgment in managing, controlling, and reporting expenses.

M. Provide in a prompt manner all required reports.

N. Keep informed of competitive activities.

O. Keep management informed of all marketing trends and conditions.

Standards of Performance Measurements

Unfortunately, many job descriptions tend to focus on responsibilities and duties while avoiding measurements of performance. A study of hundreds of job descriptions reveals that the majority are deficient in specifying measurements of performance.

Many job descriptions merely state that the person is responsible for achieving the goals and objectives as determined by the supervisor. The question arises as to what goals and objectives?

Sometimes, job descriptions simply state that the performance of the employee will be based on the degree of effectiveness in planning and decision making as determined by the supervisor. Again, what planning and decision making?

Performance measurement statements based on subjective judgments are extremely weak and difficult to support.

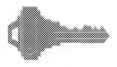

You want your job descriptions to be specific in describing standards of performance measurement. How much, how frequent, how accurate, how detailed, what degree of quantity or quality, what percent of defects, what percent of market share, etc.?

Clearly, established and specific performance standards allow employees to know how they are doing compared to expectations. A well-written standard of measurement creates a level playing field and provides a mutual understanding that leads to superior performance.

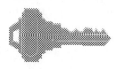
Job descriptions should include the key factors that will be used in evaluating performance. General performance measures include effectiveness in the following:

Subjective
- Planning

- Decision making

- Delegating

- Motivating

- Degree of improvement and innovation

Objective
- Achievement of goals in terms of numbers, percentages, costs, defects, etc.

The sales area provides many opportunities for clearly establishing performance standards. Setting standards for other positions is more difficult but not always insurmountable. For example, it would seem that standards in public relations would be virtually impossible. However, performance can be measured by the number of corporate or product publicity releases appearing in the media as reported by a clipping service.

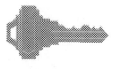
Every employee must be given a copy of a job description that needs to be continuously updated. Preparing an evaluation based on an out-of-date job description can

demoralize an employee and seriously undermine the entire appraisal process.

Computerization has made it more critical than ever for job descriptions to be continuously updated. At one time, for example, a purchasing agent could be tucked away in a small office on a manufacturing floor. Inventories and production schedules could be checked firsthand and the "in box" was the primary source of information. Today, the same purchasing agent sitting at a keyboard in the same office can instantly access the information needed to procure materials for many plants.

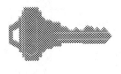 Responsibilities can be quickly and dramatically increased in today's workplace. This requires corresponding upgrades in the job description and pay classification. You need to closely monitor job descriptions to ensure ongoing accuracy.

Chapter III

◆

What To Evaluate

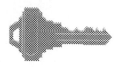

After developing job descriptions, you need to define the performance characteristics to be rated. It is important to consider both quantitative and qualitative factors.

Quantitative Analysis

Quantitative analysis is specific, measurable, and comparable in objective terms such as numbers and percentages. Ideally, two evaluators using the same quantitative data would arrive at identical conclusions. Quantitative measurements are always preferred, but many jobs do not lend themselves to this type of evaluation.

Caution must be exercised in using quantitative measurements in order to avoid too much emphasis on output, which may result in a corresponding decrease in quality.

Examples of typical quantitative rating factors are:

- Number of units produced
- Number or percent of defects
- Scrappage rate
- Percent of budget variances
- Number of sales calls
- Number of orders
- Percent of sales objective
- Share of market
- Number of promotional items placed
- Number of new accounts
- Number of lost accounts
- Expense to sales ratio

Qualitative Analysis

or characteristics

performance

Qualitative analysis includes intangible ~~personality~~ traits that are much more subjective in nature. Two evaluators using qualitative analysis could reach far different conclusions when evaluating the same person. Unlike quantitative measurements that are rarely suitable for everyone, qualitative factors do apply to virtually all human endeavors.

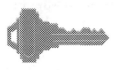

When evaluating qualitative characteristics, recognize that you are rating actual performance and not ability. A person may have the ability but fails to perform satisfactorily.

Following are some popular qualitative factors that you may wish to consider.

Sample Scale Ratings of Popular Characteristics

Accuracy

Achieving accuracy

Unsatisfactory	Below Average	Average	Good	Outstanding
number of errors is unacceptable	makes more errors than normal	meets normal accuracy standards	usually accurate with few errors	is consistent and exceptionally accurate at all times

Achievement

Carrying out responsibilities and duties

Unsatisfactory	Below Average	Average	Good	Outstanding
fails to adequately carry out basic responsibilities and duties	fails to meet normal standards of achievement	meets normal job requirements	performs consistently at a high achievement level	demonstrates exceptional ability to carry out all responsibilities and duties

Administration
Demonstrating administrative effectiveness

Unsatisfactory	Below Average	Average	Good	Outstanding
is unacceptable in carrying out basic administrative duties	fails to meet normal standards of administrative competence	demonstrates normal effectiveness in performing administrative duties	is very proficient in administering responsibilities	demonstrates distinguished performance in achieving a very high degree of administrative effectiveness

Analytical
Analyzing effectively

Unsatisfactory	Below Average	Average	Good	Outstanding
is unacceptable in analyzing critical elements of a situation	fails to meet average standards in analyzing problems and situations	demonstrates average skills when faced with analytical situations	uses sound logic and reasoning in analyzing difficult problems and situations	displays exceptional skills in thoroughly analyzing situations and taking appropriate action

Communication
Communicating with others

Unsatisfactory	Below Average	Average	Good	Outstanding
is unacceptable in communicating with others	displays poor communication skills	communicates with average skills	communicates very effectively with others	excels in highly effective communications

Competency
Demonstrating abilities and qualities

Unsatisfactory	Below Average	Average	Good	Outstanding
fails to demonstrate acceptable abilities and qualities	demonstrates a weak level of competence	is average in demonstrating abilities and qualities	demonstrates strong competence	shows exceptional abilities and qualities in carrying out responsibilities

Cooperation
Working in cooperation with others

Unsatisfactory	Below Average	Average	Good	Outstanding
is unacceptable in demonstrating cooperation	displays poor cooperation	is average in cooperating with others	displays strong cooperation skills	is exceptional and distinguished in cooperation with others at all levels

Creativity
Displaying imagination and inventiveness

Unsatisfactory	Below Average	Average	Good	Outstanding
is totally inept and unacceptable in demonstrating creativity	lacks average creative skills in developing new perspectives	displays normal creative insight and skills	initiates good conceptual ideas with practical applications	demonstrates exceptional skills in creative imagination and applications

Decision Making

Making decisions and arriving at solutions

Unsatisfactory	Below Average	Average	Good	Outstanding
fails to demonstrate acceptable performance in making decisions	is below average in making sound decisions	makes reasonable decisions in most situations	makes consistent and sound decisions based on documented facts	is extremely competent in making sound decisions and developing practical solutions

Delegating

Appointing a person authorized to speak or act for another

Unsatisfactory	Below Average	Average	Good	Outstanding
fails to delegate effectively	delegating skills are somewhat weak	generally delegates routine tasks to subordinates	is strong in delegating with clearly defined responsibility and authority	is exceptional in delegating to maximize organizational strengths

Dependability
Demonstrating reliability and trustworthiness

Unsatisfactory	Below Average	Average	Good	Outstanding
cannot be relied on to carry out responsibilities	is not always reliable in performing assigned tasks	can usually be relied on to meet schedules and deadlines	is very reliable in completing all assignments	is exceptionally reliable in carry out responsibilities to a successful conclusion

Improvement
Progressing to a better quality or condition

Unsatisfactory	Below Average	Average	Good	Outstanding
improvement fails to meet acceptable standards	needs improvement to reach average standards	is showing some progress in accomplishing improvement objectives	is making substantial progress in improving performance	shows distinguished and exceptional progress in strengthening and improving effectiveness, approaches and strategies

Initiative

Originating new ideas, methods, and approaches

Unsatisfactory	Below Average	Average	Good	Outstanding
fails to meet acceptable standards for creating new possibilities	does not meet average standards in developing new ideas and solutions	displays some creative insight in developing new concepts and techniques	can always be counted on to develop creative ideas and solutions	demonstrates exceptional skills in developing new and inventive

Innovation

Introducing new methods and procedures

Unsatisfactory	Below Average	Average	Good	Outstanding
fails to meet acceptable levels for developing innovative methods and procedures	is weak in demonstrating innovative skills	demonstrates average innovative strengths	is very innovative in developing new and better methods	excels in developing new methods, approaches, and solutions

39

Interpersonal Skills

Displaying human relations skills

Unsatisfactory	Below Average	Average	Good	Outstanding
fails to meet acceptable standards in relationships with others	is poor in developing relationships with others	gets along well with others	builds very strong working relationships	excels in developing relationships of trust and respect with supervisors, peers, and employees

Judgment

Weighing facts and premises before forming an opinion, recommendation, or course of action

Unsatisfactory	Below Average	Average	Good	Outstanding
fails to exercise acceptable judgment	cannot always be relied on to make sound judgments	makes reasonable and thoughtful judgments	can always be trusted to make good determinations based on thoughtful considerations	displays exceptional judgment in effectively diagnosing and giving careful deliberations to all situations

Knowledge

Possessing an understanding of the position and relevant conditions

Unsatisfactory	Below Average	Average	Good	Outstanding
knowledge of the position and relevant conditions is unacceptable	knowledge of responsibilities and duties does not meet average standards	is generally knowledgeable in most aspects of the position	is very knowledgeable over a wide range of position responsibilities	is exceptionally well-informed and demonstrates authoritative and comprehensive knowledge of position and field

Leadership

Demonstrating commanding authority and the capacity to lead

Unsatisfactory	Below Average	Average	Good	Outstanding
fails to show acceptable leadership qualities	is not meeting average leadership expectations	displays average leadership qualities	demonstrates strong and visionary leadership skills	demonstrates the strengths of an exceptional leader and excels in motivating and inspiring

Learning

Acquiring knowledge and skills through experience, instruction, or study

Unsatisfactory	Below Average	Average	Good	Outstanding
demonstrates unacceptable learning skills	is below average in responding to new learning situations	displays average skills in learning new methods, systems, and techniques	is good at learning and responding to new instructions, methods, and procedures	is exceptional in learning rapidly and quickly adapting to new and changing situations

Management

Managing or supervising resources

Unsatisfactory	Below Average	Average	Good	Outstanding
is unable to manage to acceptable levels	is lacking in basic management skills	applies average management principles and techniques in most situations	demonstrates strong management skills under a variety of circumstances	is exceptional in managing all available resources to successfully accomplish organizational objectives

Motivation

Motivating, stimulating, and inspiring self and others

Unsatisfactory	Below Average	Average	Good	Outstanding
fails to demonstrate acceptable motivational standards	lacks enthusiasm and a desire to achieve results	displays an average achievement drive, desire, and spirit	is strongly motivated to achieve optimal results	demonstrates an exceptional drive in fulfilling responsibilities and instilling enthusiasm

Negotiating

Conferring with another through discussion and compromise to arrive at a settlement

Unsatisfactory	Below Average	Average	Good	Outstanding
is unable to negotiate to an acceptable level	lacks average negotiating skills	is able to generally resolve conflicts and misunderstandings	is very good in working with others to resolve differing viewpoints	excels in facing confrontations and successfully arriving at a settlement without creating conflict

43

Oral Expression
Speaking proficiently

Unsatisfactory	Below Average	Average	Good	Outstanding
fails to meet acceptable standards in speech proficiency	is below average in verbal expressions	speaks with clarity and confidence	is highly articulate and very clear in verbal expressions	excels in making eminently clear verbal expressions that make dynamic impressions

Organizing
Arranging by systematic planning and united effort

Unsatisfactory	Below Average	Average	Good	Outstanding
fails to demonstrate acceptable organizing skills	is lacking in meeting average organizing skills	organizes work well	is very orderly and systematic in carrying out responsibilities	excels at a very high level of methodical and systematic planning, making a substantial contribution

Persuasiveness
Acquiring support for decisions and actions

Unsatisfactory	Below Average	Average	Good	Outstanding
is not meeting acceptable persuasion level	is lacking in persuasion skills	demonstrates normal persuasive skills	is able to very effectively persuade	is distinguished in acquiring support for decisions and actions

Planning
Formulating strategies, tactics, and action plans to achieve results

Unsatisfactory	Below Average	Average	Good	Outstanding
does not meet acceptable planning standards	lacks adequate planning skills	plans effectively in most situations	is very proficient in formulating strategically sound plans	excels in planning appropriate strategies to arrive at successful solutions

Potential
Possessing unrealized and undeveloped capabilities

Unsatisfactory	Below Average	Average	Good	Outstanding
demonstrates no potential for growth	shows little potential for growth or advancement	displays average potential for growth	is a high potential employee	is exceptionally capable of assuming greater responsibility at a higher level position

Presentation Skills
Offering a subject for consideration and acceptance

Unsatisfactory	Below Average	Average	Good	Outstanding
fails to meet acceptable presentation levels	lacks in demonstrating presentation skills	makes effective presentations in most situations	demonstrates strong presentation skills in all situations	excels in making powerful presentations with maximum impact

Prioritizing
Making arrangements in order of priority

Unsatisfactory	Below Average	Average	Good	Outstanding
is unable to meet acceptable levels of prioritizing	is lacking in making priority determinations	keeps situations in proper perspective	is above average in prioritizing tasks, activities, and objectives	excels in distinguishing between low and high priority activities

Problem Solving
Finding a solution to a difficult or perplexing situation

Unsatisfactory	Below Average	Average	Good	Outstanding
fails to meet acceptable standards in solving problems	is lacking in problem-solving skills	is able to generally solve problems	is unusually decisive in handling difficult problems	excels in identifying, analyzing, and finding solutions to a problem

Productivity
Producing in abundance or degree of effectiveness

Unsatisfactory	Below Average	Average	Good	Outstanding
fails to meet acceptable output standards	produces at less than normal output levels	produces at an average achievement level	maintains unusually high output	is exceptional in producing far more than expected

Professionalism
Conforming to professional standards

Unsatisfactory	Below Average	Average	Good	Outstanding
is unacceptable in meeting professional standards	is lacking in demonstrating professional skills	displays an average degree of professional knowledge and skills	demonstrates a very high level of professional performance	is distinguished in demonstrating an exceptional mastery of professional skills

Quality
Achieving a degree of excellence

Unsatisfactory	Below Average	Average	Good	Outstanding
fails to meet acceptable quality levels	is lacking in meeting average quality standards	achieves average quality levels in most situations	is highly committed to providing superior quality	is exceptional in striving for perfection and achieving the highest quality

Resourcefulness
Drawing effectively upon resources to achieve objectives

Unsatisfactory	Below Average	Average	Good	Outstanding
is unable to make acceptable use of resources	lacks effectiveness in demonstrating resourcefulness	makes average use of personal and organizational resources	is able to achieve success when confronted with limited resources	is outstanding in utilizing all available resources to overcome the most difficult situations

Responsibility

Assuming accountability for obligations, duties and actions

Unsatisfactory	Below Average	Average	Good	Outstanding
fails to accept responsibility	somewhat lacking in accepting responsiblity	is average in accepting and carrying out responsibilities	is strong in seeking, accepting and fulfilling responsibilities	is exceptional in assuming ultimate responsibilities

Selling Skills

Influencing or persuading the transfer of ownership to another

Unsatisfactory	Below Average	Average	Good	Outstanding
fails to display acceptable selling skills	demonstrates weak selling abilities	displays adequate selling skills	consistently demonstrates effective selling abilities	is exceptional in demonstrating strong selling skills and exceeding sales expectations

Supervision

Managing and directing the efforts of others

Unsatisfactory	Below Average	Average	Good	Outstanding
is failing to meet the standards expected of a supervisor	is somewhat lacking in the effective supervision of employees	is able to generally manage employees to achieve goals and objectives	is very good at maximizing the performance of people and equipment	is exceptional in supervising and leading others to achieve optimum results

Tact and Diplomacy

Dealing with others under difficult situations without offending

Unsatisfactory	Below Average	Average	Good	Outstanding
is unable to demonstrate acceptable skills in conflict situations	lacks poise and tact when encountering difficult situations with others	makes tactful and appropriate responses	is very good at saying and doing the right thing without offending others	demonstrates exceptional and polished skills when dealing with others in difficult situations

Team Skills

Participating in the joint and coordinated action of a group

Unsatisfactory	Below Average	Average	Good	Outstanding
is unable to meet acceptable standards in team efforts	is lacking as a participant in team efforts	demonstrates average participation in team efforts	is a strong member in any team activities	is exceptional in making valuable contributions to all team efforts

Technical Skills

Applying knowledge of industrial, mechanical or applied sciences

Unsatisfactory	Below Average	Average	Good	Outstanding
does not meet expected technical competence	technical knowledge and application is weak	displays average technical knowledge and skills	demonstrates strong technical competence	demonstrates an exceptionally high level of technical competence

Versatility

Demonstrating competence in many diverse areas

Unsatisfactory	Below Average	Average	Good	Outstanding
is unable to demonstrate acceptable and diversified skills	is somewhat lacking in displaying capabilities for diversified assignments	can usually maintain essential operations while covering a variety of functions	is good at performing a broad range of assignments and providing back-up support in many positions	is a distinguished performer in competently providing excellent organizational support in many areas

Writing Skills

Communicaing in writing

Unsatisfactory	Below Average	Average	Good	Outstanding
writing skills are unacceptable	fails to meet average writing proficiency	genaerally displays normal writing proficiency	demonstrates strong writing skills	is exceptional in writing with clarity, consistently and effectiveness

 You want to select qualitative characteristics using common sense. Negotiating, for example, is meaningless to a file clerk. However, it is critical to a labor relations manager or a salesperson.

Chapter IV

◆

When to Evaluate

The time for conducting performance reviews varies considerably by company and organization. Two of the most common evaluation times are the annual date of employment and a standard time for everyone. Special and more frequent times are usually scheduled for new employees.

Annual Date of Employment

Evaluating personnel on the anniversary of their hiring date is becoming increasing undesirable in view of the fast pace of today's organizational life with its mergers, acquisitions, consolidations, downsizing, and executive mobility.

The disadvantages of evaluating everyone on a person's anniversary are many. It is conceivable that an employee could be evaluated every year by a different supervisor using a different form and thereby destroying all continuity. Furthermore, job responsibilities within a department or division can change dramatically within a year's time, making comparisons with other employees meaningless.

Annual Standard Period

Appraising everyone in an organization during the same time period is the fairest and best method. A standard appraisal time provides a snapshot of the company at any given time similar to a balance sheet.

With a set period for evaluating, all organizational structures, sales, earnings, budgets, and rumors are in place and applicable to everyone. Fall has traditionally been a popular time for evaluations. Budgets are finalized and the organization is gearing up to meet the challenges for the coming year.

Some companies actually rate in December. For many firms, sales and production schedules are sluggish in December and managers often have ample free time. Companies frequently shut down under union contracts, paperwork often decreases, and the organization is not operating at peak efficiency. A slowdown in operations allows time to reflect on the past year and plan for the new one.

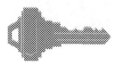
All factors considered, fall is usually the best time to evaluate. Early in the week is also preferred for interviews. Managers should not make it appear that they do not wish to see employees during the remainder of the week and need a weekend to avoid them. Appraising in December is generally not advisable because appraisals may be influenced by the jovial mood of the holiday season.

New employees are often appraised at three, six and twelve months using brief and special forms.

Chapter V

◆

Designing the Form

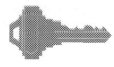 You do not want to impair the effectiveness of an appraisal form by making it too long and complex. Harried managers will recognize a lengthy form as overkill and will quickly develop a negative attitude toward the entire program.

Keeping Forms Concise and Simple

A form no longer than three pages is generally suitable for virtually all positions. A concise form will not generate negative reactions and will usually allow managers to make more thoughtful, concentrated, and accurate ratings. In the world of evaluations, a scale of five is the most common. Five stars are used to rate restaurants, movies, and books. The scale of five allows an average rating to be placed directly in the middle with space on either side for less than average or more than average ratings.

The author has reviewed many hundreds of evaluation forms. Many of these forms have been prepared by experts in the HR field. Surprisingly, the layouts of these forms vary widely. It is clear that no single design is suitable for all organizations.

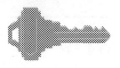 You always want to include clear instructions on the form and provide a method for scoring, which will be discussed in a later chapter.

Narrative Style Forms

Some companies use a narrative or essay type of form. The evaluator is only required to write a paragraph or two describing the employee's strengths, weaknesses, and potential for advancement. The author has seen forms where the evaluator has written comments in exceptionally large handwriting in order to fill space. The disadvantage of the essay-type form is that it is highly subjective and does not lend itself to comparative analysis.

Evaluations by Objectives

Other forms measure performance by percent of goals or objectives achieved. This type of evaluation is extremely difficult because most jobs do not lend themselves to clearly stated and objective goals.

Sample Rating Forms

Following are a number of the more common designs using the judgment characteristic as an example:

Forced Rating by Ranking Categories

Exercises Sound Judgment

❑   ❑   ❑   ❑   ❑
1   2   3   4   5

Definitions

    1: Low—lacking in performance

    2: Satisfactory—somewhat lacking in performance

    3: Fair—fulfills essential job requirements

    4: Good—exceeds normal job performance

    5: High—demonstrates outstanding performance

Forced Rating by Reversed Ranking Categories

Some forms reverse the normal horizontal rankings by placing excellent performance first. The style is similar to a proofreading technique of reading backwards, which requires greater thought and unconventional thinking. Following is an example:

Exercises Sound Judgment

❑   ❑   ❑   ❑   ❑
4   3   2   1   0

    4: Excellent

    3: Good

    2: Fair

    1: Poor

    0: Unsatisfactory

Forced Ranking by Frequency Category

Exercises Sound Judgment

❑	❑	❑	❑	❑
0	1	2	3	4

0: Never

1: Seldom

2: Sometimes

3: Usually

4: Always

Forced Ranking by Descriptive Categories and Essay

One of the most popular layouts is to place a brief description of performance under the relative score ratings. This type of form offers one of the best approaches to accurately measuring performance. It provides a practical method of ranking overall performance in quartiles. The descriptive examples also increase accuracy by requiring raters to think about the relative meaning of each rating as shown below:

Exercises Sound Judgment

❑	❑	❑	❑	❑
0	1	2	3	4

0: Fails to exercise sound judgment

1: Sometimes neglects to give careful thought to judgments

2: Displays average judgment

3: Consistently makes sound judgments

4: Exercises exceptional judgment in all situations

Comments:

_____

_____

_____

_____

_____

_____

The evaluator is required to provide additional comments for each characteristic.

Single Definition Plus Scale Rating and Essay

Judgment

Demonstrates ability to arrive at sound decisions using factual and analytical reasoning

❏	❏	❏	❏	❏	❏	❏	❏	❏	❏
1	2	3	4	5	6	7	8	9	10

1: Unsatisfactory

2: Very poor

3: Poor

4: Below average

5: Average

6: Good

7: Very good

8: Outstanding

9: Exceptional

10: Distinguished

Comments:

_____

_____

_____

_____

_____

_____

_____

_____

Average, typical, and satisfactory performance is 5 on the above scale. The mid-point allows adequate space to rate superior and inferior performance. The large number of possible points makes this form especially desirable when rating a large number of people with the same job description such as a sales force.

Every characteristic must have a written explanation in addition to the scale ratings. Very high or very low ratings must be especially detailed and supported with substantial justification.

Combination Scale Rating, Definitive Questions, and Essay

The most effective design in the author's opinion includes both a scale rating, definitive questions, and required essay comments. A system of this type allows detailed ranking of score ratings and also requires the evaluator to justify and elaborate on the ratings in writing. The broad range of scale numbers is also suitable for large groups.

Carefully worded questions make it clear what is to be evaluated. Following are examples of this layout covering a variety of characteristics:

Point values:

1: Unsatisfactory

2: Very poor

3: Poor

4: Below average

5: Average

6: Good

7: Very good

8: Outstanding

9: Exceptional

10: Distinguished

Productivity

Does the employee exhibit industry and initiative in completing assignments and responsibilities on time and achieve significant results? Does the employee plan and organize effectively in order to properly utilize work time, services of others, equipment, and materials?

Comments:

_____

_____

_____

_____

_____

_____

_____

Professional Knowledge and Applicable Skills

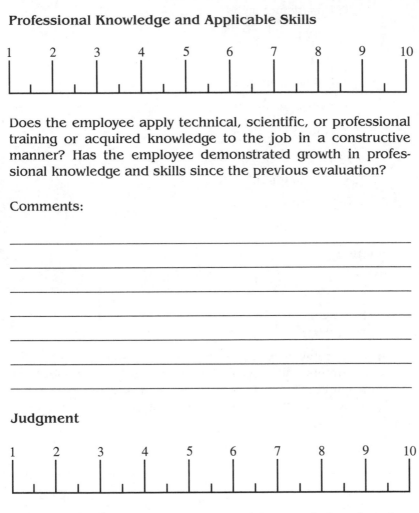

Does the employee apply technical, scientific, or professional training or acquired knowledge to the job in a constructive manner? Has the employee demonstrated growth in professional knowledge and skills since the previous evaluation?

Comments:

_____

_____

_____

_____

_____

_____

_____

Judgment

Does the employee make sound decisions and show imagination and inventiveness in improving situations, eliminating that which is unnecessary and acting upon that which is important? Consider formulating new ideas, utilizing facts and past experience and the number of contributions the employee has made for improving methods, systems, procedures, and the number accepted.

Comments:

_____

_____

_____

_____

_____

_____

_____

Written and Oral Expression

| 1 | 2 | 3 | 4 | 5 | 6 | 7 | 8 | 9 | 10 |

Does the employee initiate and provide clear and concise communications including reports? Consider clear and logical expressions in both written and spoken language.

Comments:

_____

_____

_____

_____

_____

_____

Improvement

| 1 | 2 | 3 | 4 | 5 | 6 | 7 | 8 | 9 | 10 |

Has the employee followed suggestions for improvement made during previous appraisals? Has there been any improvement? If not, why?

Comments:

_____

_____

_____

_____

_____

_____

Managerial Effectiveness (where applicable)

| 1 | 2 | 3 | 4 | 5 | 6 | 7 | 8 | 9 | 10 |

Consider performance in planning, organizing, controlling, directing, and delegating. Does the person handle responsibilities well? Consider training and guidance given to employees, along with motivating and leadership performance.

Comments:

_____

_____

_____

_____

_____

_____

_____

Overall Appraisal

Summarize the employee's all-around performance based on the composite of the individual appraisal factors.

Comments:

_____

_____

_____

_____

_____

_____

_____

Recommendations

Enter below suggestions for increasing the employee's contribution and growth potential.

_____

_____

_____

_____

_____

_____

_____

Nearly all forms require the employee to sign a statement similar to, "I have reviewed this appraisal and discussed the content with my immediate superior. My signature means that I have been advised of my performance and does not necessarily imply that I agree with the overall appraisal or its contents."

Other forms also provide an opportunity for the employee to provide optional comments as follows:

"If the employee wishes, any comments or explanations (agreement or disagreement) concerning the content of this appraisal may be entered in the space below."

_____

_____

_____

_____

_____

_____

The form normally concludes with space for the evaluator's signature, along with additional reviewers as follows:

Completed by _____   Date _____

Reviewed by   _____   Date _____

Reviewed by   _____   Date _____

You want to print the form on high quality paper to convey the image associated with an important company document.

Performance appraisal forms at all levels need to be continuously monitored. Revised forms are warranted whenever there are significant changes in the organization, marketplace, or company systems. You need to clearly review all forms before each evaluation period to ensure their accuracy and reliability.

Distributing Appraisal Forms

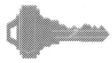

Although appraisal forms are prepared by HR personnel, the actual distribution needs to be downward through line management. The completed forms should be returned upward through line management with a senior executive returning them to the HR department. Distribution of forms is time-consuming and employees need to be aware that their completed appraisal will travel upward from their supervisor to a manager, to a director, to a vice-president, and perhaps to the president and then to HR.

Maintaining Confidentiality

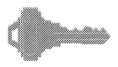

You must also recognize the important need for confidentiality in dealing with performance appraisals. You do not want an employee's evaluation lying on your desk or appearing on your computer screen while other people are wandering in and out of your office. You also do not want to discuss evaluations without applying the time-tested "need to know" principle. Nothing can more quickly undermine a sound program than having rumors of someone's evaluation spreading around the work area.

With job mobility at record levels, employees are more comfortable discussing employment issues with others. Employees who compare notes and find that an equal performer received a higher rating and a larger pay increase can quickly demoralize an organization.

Clearly, evaluation forms need to be maintained in a restricted area and computer access must be highly controlled.

Although you may feel extremely competent in all areas of HR, you need to have your final appraisal form reviewed by legal counsel.

Chapter VI

◆

How to Rate

Assume you are the general manager or owner of a big league baseball team and it's player evaluation time. You need to merely gather your statistical data and measure the number of hits, runs batted in, home runs, strikeouts, errors, etc. In the statistical world of baseball, evaluations are a piece of cake. Unfortunately, appraisals are not as simple in the real world.

Managers and employees often approach appraisals with conflicting objectives. Today's managers are often under pressure from higher management to limit salary and wage increases. In many cases, managers are reluctant to give high ratings because they are operating under strict programs that do not allow for variances in budgeted compensation increases.

On the other hand, employees wish to receive high overall ratings, which they hope will result in sizable pay increases.

Checking a series of boxes may seem almost clerical to some managers. However, to an employee, it may be the difference between buying a used car or a new car or moving into a larger apartment.

Keep in mind that a common objective is that both the manager and employee wish to improve performance.

Always rate an individual's performance on the basis of previously established measurement standards rather than in competition with other employees who are performing similar functions. If a department has a truly outstanding employee with exceptional skills, it is not valid to use this employee as a comparison standard. Of course, it would also follow that an unsatisfactory employee would not serve as a comparison.

Confine your ratings to the period since the last appraisal. Accomplishments and successes in the previous appraisal do not carry over into the current appraisal.

Performance is always evaluated on what has taken place. Merit pay increases, in particular, should never be based on promises of future performance.

Avoid Confusing Activity With Accomplishment

Be careful to avoid confusing activity with accomplishment. Some employees are always in constant motion, sending e-mails, telephoning, and attending meetings. These busy bodies often have desks that are cluttered with paper. They are on the car phone before their car is out of the driveway. They often arrive early, stay late, and convey the image of a true and dedicated employee.

The author once knew an executive who arrived an hour before the office opened and walked the halls turning on all the lights. The obvious intent was to make higher executives believe that everyone on the floor was also in early and working hard at their desks.

Rate Performance, Not Personality

Do not let your own personality influence ratings. As a manager, you may consistently arrive at meetings about ten minutes before the appointed time. One of your subordinates may always arrive one minute before the scheduled time. Just because your behavior and style may be different is no reason to let it influence ratings. Remember, you are rating performance and not personality.

Managers often have a gut feeling about the performance of a particular person. These managers often make the mistake of merely using an appraisal form to justify their general feelings without giving consideration to specific performance characteristics.

Other managers are only concerned with bottom-line results. If department turnover is low, budgets are met and nobody in management is complaining, they could care less about planning, organizing, and evaluating. These managers may treat appraisals as a mechanical process to be quickly disposed of. This approach is not fair to the employee who does not know what areas need to be improved for achieving greater responsibility and success.

 Complete your appraisals in draft form and set them aside for a day or two. By going back and reviewing them again, you are likely to have second thoughts or discover needed corrections.

Most firms require the appraiser to enter comments on an overall appraisal. It's easy to merely check a box, but to substantiate your rating in writing requires more thought and attention.

Following are examples of unacceptable and acceptable comments:

Unacceptable:
You are doing a fairly good job and get along well with customers but need to improve your selling effectiveness. You excel in your golf outings with customers. Your expenses are above-average and should be reduced. Otherwise, you are doing OK.

Acceptable
You have excellent relations with many key accounts. However, your performance in meeting 67 percent of your sales objective through the first six months of the year needs to be improved. Your call order ratio of 27 to 1 should be improved to a target of 8 to 1. Expenses for the first six months exceeded our budgeted amount by 14 percent and corrective action is required to bring you within your budgeted amount by year-end. I will review your performance with you at the end of the third quarter.

You have the potential to become a leading sales representative by strengthening your selling skills. To assist you in this effort, I am recommending that you attend a nationally recognized sales training program that will be most beneficial to your career.

Using the Sandwich Approach

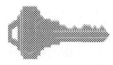

You can make effective use of the time-proven sandwich approach by describing both strengths and weak areas in need of improvement, followed by compliments. With this method, you provide positive strokes, highlight areas in need of improvement, and then end on a positive note. This method allows you to get your message across but does not destroy the morale and incentive of an employee.

The Bell Shaped Curve

It has long been accepted that the measurement of nearly all human traits follows a bell-shaped curve. The majority of individuals will appear in the middle of the curve, with fewer persons at each end as shown below.

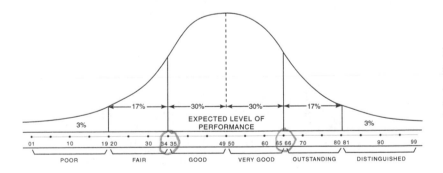

Ideally, about 60 percent of your ratings will fall between 35 and 65. The remaining ratings will be distributed at each end as illustrated.

The bell-shaped curve concept is often in conflict with managers who believe that their department is totally different because only top performers are hired. While it may very well be a superior department, variances in performance will still occur although perhaps at a higher level.

Managers who are cautioned about rating too high often respond by saying, "I only hire outstanding personnel in the first place." Imagine what would happen if everyone in an organization claimed that only superior people are on their staff. Remember, the bell-shaped curve applies to every group even if the bell is moved upward on the scale.

Rating a poor performer as average diminishes the value of the appraisal system and is unfair to others in the organization. Inflated ratings actually devaluate the evaluations given to truly outstanding performers.

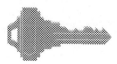 Unless the policy of your organization requires evaluations at different times, it is far better to appraise all of your employees during the same general time period.

For example, you would not want to be rated during the days when your boss is experiencing serious personal problems. A boss who is preparing for major surgery will likely be in a different mood compared to a time of taking delivery on a beautiful new sailboat.

Many managers procrastinate when it comes to appraisals. They often wait until the last moment and rush through the process.

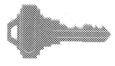 You want to take steps to promptly complete the evaluations of employees. If a teacher is observed in a classroom, for example, the ratings should be discussed shortly thereafter while interest and memory retention is high.

By taking prompt and professional action, you can create a positive environment and help reduce the number of employees who complain about those "darn" appraisals. The manager who takes prompt action impresses both superiors and employees.

From personal experience, I believe it's best to complete appraisals at a site other than the workplace. You want to be in a comfortable and relaxed setting and not be bothered by interruptions.

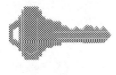

Prior to rating, remind yourself that you have both a moral and legal obligation to be objective and fair. Your rating should be based solely on performance and independent of personal bias or prejudice.

Be Aware of Rating Influences

To rate fairly and effectively, make yourself aware of the following key factors that can influence your ratings:

1. *The halo effect:*
   The tendency of an evaluator to rate a person good or poorly on all characteristics based on an experience or knowledge involving only one dimension.

2. *Leniency tendency:*
   A tendency toward evaluating all persons as outstanding and to give inflated ratings rather than true assessments of performance.

3. *Strictness tendency:*
   The opposite of the leniency tendency; that is, a bias toward rating all persons at the low end of the scale and a tendency to be over-demanding or critical.

4. *Average tendency:*
   A tendency to evaluate every person as average regardless of major differences in performance.

With regard to the leniency tendency, the trend in American organizational life is toward more leniency in all aspects of the workplace. Flexible hours, work at home, casual wear, and child care facilities are all contributing to a new work environment. You want to take special measures to ensure that the leniency tendency does not carry over into performance reviews.

Ratings may also be influenced by other factors such as the following:

1. Close proximity in the work area

2. Distant employee with little personal contact

3. Common interests with employee and close association in areas such as sports, politics, education, car pooling, etc.

Considering Uncontrollable Factors

 You also need to carefully consider outside factors beyond the control of employees when completing appraisals. Depending on the field, examples of external considerations that can understandingly affect performance are:

- Strikes

- Fires

- Raw material shortages

- Equipment and machinery changes

- Currency fluctuations

- Price increases

- Product shortages

- Changing product demand

- New competition

- Abnormal weather

- New programs, policies, and procedures

- Employee turnover

- Legislative actions

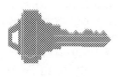 Always take into consideration uncontrollable and varying circumstances especially when using a standard form to evaluate distant employees. For example, assume you are the sales manager in the following conversation:

Sales Manager:

I am disappointed in your sales for the past year. Your sales were down 14 percent while our national sales were up 8 percent. You simply are not carrying your share, and I had to rate you accordingly. You definitely need to improve your selling skills.

Salesperson:

You are correct. My sales were down last year. However, did you take into consideration that my state does not have a periodic vehicle inspection program like all my surrounding states? As a result of recently passed legislation, I am now at a severe disadvantage and believe a sales decrease of only 14 percent is outstanding in view of current market conditions. My state does not require motorists to periodically meet pollution standards thereby affecting a demand for our products. I am simply not on a level playing field, and your comments are not fair.

Sales Manager:
> Gee, I guess you are right. I frankly did not weigh the situation in completing your appraisal. I'll have to fill out another form and get back to you on this.

A conversation such as the foregoing can destroy morale and seriously undermine an otherwise sound evaluation program. You need to consider all variables, especially when evaluating distant employees.

 As with all employment matters, you want to avoid any references to age, gender, race, religion, disabilities, etc., in the evaluation process. You may suspect that an employee is an alcoholic, stealing company property, or encountering marital problems but do not discuss or enter your thoughts into the company record. Anything you record may be subject to a court test at a later date and must be defensible.

It is also important to distinguish behavior from performance. Employee A may be friendly, outgoing, always smiling, and the best liked person in the plant. Employee B may be quiet, a true introvert, and a classic loner. Yet, employee B may have the best production output and the lowest scrappage rate of anyone in the plant. Assuming the job descriptions and production measurement standards are identical, employee B has earned a higher rating.

Too much emphasis on a rigid appraisal form can be misleading and unfair in certain situations. For example, an employee may be rated average in communications, decision making, and delegating. The person may frequently miss meetings, submit late reports, and often leave work early to play golf.

However, the same person may be extremely creative and may have, for example, submitted a single idea that generated millions of dollars in corporate profits. This person would score low on an appraisal form having many rating factors and completed in strict conformance to standard instructions. Clearly, management must sometimes take a broad and flexible view of a rigid appraisal program.

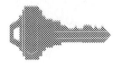

Raters using a standard form to evaluate many persons at the same level need to give special consideration to newer employees. An experienced person will understandably have greater job knowledge than an employee who is relatively new in the identical position. A newer employee can be fairly rated on the degree of progress based on the amount of training and ability to learn.

The best evaluation program will not succeed unless managers and supervisors are thoroughly trained. You need to place a high priority on training evaluators to properly implement the appraisal program. A number of excellent materials and videos are available on conducting appraisals, and they can prove to be a very wise investment. Remember that the ability to testify that all management personnel have been trained in proper methods of evaluations can be a powerful plus in litigation.

Chapter VII

◆

Scoring

OK, all your managers and supervisors have been trained in the essentials of performance appraisals. All of the forms have been completed. What next?

Employees in the same general classification of responsibility need to be ranked. The ranking procedure can be extremely complicated or simple and fair.

Here is a simple and fair approach to ranking. Assume you are using a scoring system of one to five as follows:

Unsatisfactory	Average	Good	Very Good	Distinguished

You need to assign a point value to each of the incremental ratings as shown below:

Unsatisfactory	Average	Good	Very Good	Distinguished
0 points	1 point	2 points	3 points	4 points

 A lot of common sense is involved in assigning scoring values to appraisal forms. Accuracy, for example, is much more critical when evaluating an accountant

compared to a receptionist. In such situations, you want to assign higher point values to reflect relatively more important responsibilities. As another example, job descriptions for selling positions generally place greater emphasis on developing new accounts than on administrative duties. The evaluation form would be weighted to reflect this relative importance as follows:

Sales Representative

Administration

Unsatisfactory	Average	Good	Very Good	Distinguished
0 points	1 point	2 points	3 points	4 points

Developing New Accounts

Unsatisfactory	Average	Good	Very Good	Distinguished
0 points	2 points	4 points	6 points	8 points

By adding the total points for each characteristic on each form, you will arrive at a total number for each employee. Next, rank all employees from high to low based on the total for each employee as follows:

No. of Points	Representative
146	Jane Doe 1
145	John Doe 2
143	Jane Doe 3
141	John Doe 4
141	Jane Doe 5
139	John Doe 6
137	Jane Doe 7

136	John Doe 8
134	Jane Doe 9
130	John Doe 10
123	Jane Doe 11
122	John Doe 12
120	Jane Doe 13
117	John Doe 14
115	Jane Doe 15
110	John Doe 16
103	Jane Doe 17
101	John Doe 18
97	Jane Doe 19
92	John Doe 20

Next, divide the rankings into four equal groups or quartiles as follows:

	146	Jane Doe 1
	145	John Doe 2
1st Quartile	143	Jane Doe 3
	141	John Doe 4
	141	Jane Doe 5
	139	John Doe 6
	137	Jane Doe 7
2nd Quartile	136	John Doe 8
	134	Jane Doe 9
	130	John Doe 10
	123	Jane Doe 11
	122	John Doe 12
3rd Quartile	120	Jane Doe 13
	117	John Doe 14
	115	Jane Doe 15

	110	John Doe 16
	103	Jane Doe 17
4th Quartile	101	John Doe 18
	97	Jane Doe 19
	92	John Doe 20

The system can only be used in situations where individuals have similar positions and are rated on identical forms. Management, administrative, clerical, technical, and salespersons are examples of groups that are commonly scored and ranked separately.

By ranking into quartiles, it is easy to compare relative performance and assign compensation by appropriate groups. This system is fair, honest, and statistically indisputable.

Chapter VIII

◆

The Interview

Most people think of performance appraisals in terms of a rating form. They fail to realize that forms are merely one phase of the evaluation process. In many ways, the interview is the most critical element of the appraisal program.

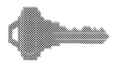 You want to be continuously evaluating and coaching employees. Rather than maintaining a "tickler file," a professional manager promptly handles problems as they occur. No performance deficiencies are bottled up to be uncorked during the review interview.

By maintaining open communications, a strong manager develops a pattern of trust with employees. As a result, employees have a pretty good idea of how they are doing and do not experience sweaty palms and anxiety at the annual appraisal interview.

Employee's Interview Preparation

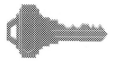 From an employee's viewpoint, it's also important to prepare for the appraisal interview. Employees need to anticipate possible

problems and be prepared to respond in a
positive and enthusiastic manner.

Before the interview, employees should review comments
from the previous appraisal and concentrate on their improvements and accomplishments. Consider all factors beyond your
control that may have affected your performance. It's easy for
a busy supervisor to overlook both your contributions and un-
controllable factors. A friendly reminder is always appropriate.
Do not be afraid to toot your own horn.

Supervisor's Interview Preparation

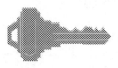

Successful managers recognize that prepa-
ration is the key to a mutually beneficial interview. Skilled managers will review the
completed appraisal form, consider constructive criticism, anticipate possible objections, and plan improvement objectives.

Following is a preappraisal interview checklist:

Preappraisal Interview Checklist

1: Gather all materials, records, and supporting documents that may be needed.

2: Anticipate possible problems and objections.

3: Review the company handbook on policy issues
that may arise.

4: Plan goals and objectives for needed improvements including specific target dates.

5: Plan for monitoring and follow-up discussions.

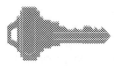

Scheduling the interview several days in advance along with the appointment time is
essential. The early part of the week is usually the best time. Avoid Fridays that convey

the image that you are glad it's over and do not wish to see the employee until after a cooling off period of a couple of days.

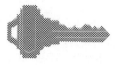

Conduct your interviews in a neutral setting such as a conference room where there will be no interruptions. Conducting an interview in the supervisor's office surrounded by symbols of power can be very intimidating. Keep in mind that both the evaluator and the employee are both employees of the company.

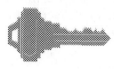

Another tip is for the supervisor to sit side-by-side with the employee rather than across a desk or table. A desk or table serves as a psychological barrier; whereas adjacent seating reinforces a feeling of mutual interest and support. The situation is similar to a waiter or waitress who kneels down while taking your food order, in order to establish a friendly relationship.

The professional literature varies on the best method of opening the interview. Some experts believe that small talk should be completely avoided and others believe it is most appropriate.

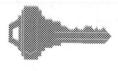

Ask the employee to discuss their strengths and compliment them wherever there is agreement. If the employee finds it difficult to discuss their assets, you should stimulate the discussion by pointing out observed strengths. I have found that employees are more likely to discuss their shortcomings after their strengths have been recognized.

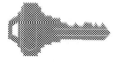

The three key words in the interview are honesty, openness, and trust. A strong manager provides employees in advance with a copy of the appraisal form and requests that they complete it and bring it to the interview. Providing the form prior to the interview reduces anxiety and leads to a constructive discussion.

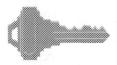 You should first ask employees about their self-appraisal ratings, then review your ratings. Asking questions requires the employee to think and gives you an opportunity to observe and measure objectivity. When you tell an employee about their performance your observations can be interpreted as criticism and the employee may quickly adopt a protective or defensive position.

Another approach is to begin the interview by informing the employee that you are going to review their ratings and offer any needed coaching to improve performance.

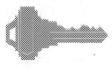 It is critical that you listen and not dominate the interview. A time-proven method is to ask many questions and listen. However, listening too much carries the danger that the employee may turn the tables and evaluate the manager. You always want to listen, but do not lose control.

 Keep the interview job-related and do not go on the defensive. Concentrate on facts and not on opinions or feelings.

Do not use the interview to discuss compensation, fringe benefits, or promotions that should be covered in separate meetings.

Unless performance is totally unacceptable, avoid negative words such as failure and unsatisfactory. Instead, emphasize improvement or much-needed improvement.

Do not discuss performance in general terms or opinions. Employees deeply resent such statements as "you need to communicate better" or "your work habits need to be improved."

Instead, be specific with your constructive criticism such as "you need to communicate better with other departments at the weekly staff meetings." As another example, "your work habits in submitting your expense reports and budget variances on time need to be improved."

Appraisal interviews too often regress into a discussion of the past. You want to focus on the future and emphasize solutions, not problems.

Handling the Problem Employee

In situations where serious performance problems are present, you must be especially prepared. For example, if a production scheduling person takes issue with a low rating, you want to quickly produce several previously discussed letters from customers complaining about back orders. If improvement is not forthcoming, the employee needs to be informed that serious consequences including possible termination will follow. All discussions of this type need to be kept strictly confidential.

Nothing can destroy a supervisor's credibility faster than criticizing an employee without having factual information. For example, consider the following discussion:

Employee:
> I am getting the impression that you are not especially pleased with my work.

Manager:
> As a matter of fact, I am not.

Employee:
> Well, what's the problem?

Manager:
> I feel that your project management needs substantial improvement.

Employee:
> You've got to be kidding. This was the one part of my job where I sure didn't expect any complaints. Can you give me some specific examples of the problem?

Manager:
> Oh-uh- I really can't give you specifics. I just have a feeling that you need to do much better in handling your projects.

WOW! . . . A conversation such as the foregoing will completely destroy all trust and credibility in the employment relationship.

If the interview turns negative, it is imperative that you keep calm and professional.

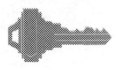 When improvement is seriously needed, you want to set performance goals, explain the type of support that will be made available, and set a follow-up timetable.

Action plans need to be put into writing either on the appraisal form itself or in a follow-up communication.

Sometimes weak managers try to avoid confrontations and anxiety by downplaying the importance of appraisals. For example:

Manager:

> By the way, I've got a bunch of appraisal forms from HR that I need to fill out. It's no big deal, but I've got to turn them in. I'll drop by next week because you will need to sign yours.

The employee who accepts this kind of treatment will likely be the same person who complains about not getting a good raise. It reminds me of a plaque that I once had in my office that stated: "The Loudest Boos Always Come From Those in the Free Seats!"

Positive Reinforcement

Some managers believe they can improve performance by using bitter criticism and tongue-lashing. In fact, negative approaches can lead to employee withdrawal, a feeling of worthlessness, and a lack of motivation.

Consequently, you can achieve higher levels of performance by reinforcing employees when they perform exceptionally well. Reinforcement can be in many forms: a word of appreciation, compliments in front of others, and money. You want to recognize the tremendous value of positive reinforcement and use it effectively at every opportunity.

With employees more openly sharing information, power managers know that a good reputation for handling appraisals—especially the interview—is a real tribute. Consider the following conversation between two employees:

George:

> Tell me . . . how did your appraisal go?

Michael:

    I wish you didn't ask. The boss really let off steam. I was criticized for nearly everything but received virtually no compliments.

George:

    That sounds familiar. I got the same treatment. I was sure you would receive many compliments and gratitude for developing the new budget program.

Michael:

    I have had just about enough of this garbage. Maybe it's time to look for another job.

George:

    I feel the same way.

Obviously you want to build morale, not destroy it.

Before making any critical comments, it's always smart to ask if there are any reasons for poor performance in a specific area because there may be legitimate causes. Always give employees an opportunity to provide feedback concerning circumstances that may be unknown to you. For example, "My budget variances have not been submitted on time because the statements from the accounting department are always received after your deadline."

The managers who most dread the formal interview are the same persons who do not maintain open communication with employees. Problems must be nipped in the bud and not handled during the appraisal interview that could be as long as a year away.

Following is what can occur in the absence of open communication:

Manager:

In the administrative area I gave you only a three.

Employee:

A three, that's only average. Why would you give me a three?

Manager:

Well, you have failed on several occasions during the past year to submit your monthly reports on time. Moreover, you have never responded to my e-mails concerning your high expenses.

Employee:

Gee, thanks a lot. Why in the hell didn't you say something earlier about my late reports. I simply felt that you were so busy that you never got around to reviewing them until several weeks after the time they were due. With regard to expenses, I mentioned to you in the hallway after our last sales meeting that my expenses are going to be higher because two of my largest accounts have relocated 200 miles down state and will require more travel and overnight accommodations. I had the impression that you clearly understood the situation and that no formal report was necessary.

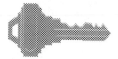 The foregoing exchange completely undermines a successful appraisal program interview and creates a total lack of trust and understanding. You want to make every effort to keep open and ongoing communications with all of your employees.

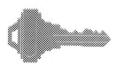 Impress upon your employees that evaluation is a continuous process and not just a once or twice a year formal procedure.

You may have a dozen or more interviews to conduct. It can easily become a routine and mechanical process.

Remember that the employee has only one interview. It may be one of the few opportunities to sit face-to-face with a supervisor.

 You want to always end the interview on a positive note and ask the person to sign the form, which usually states that it has been reviewed and does not necessarily indicate agreement or disagreement.

The ideal interview will end on a feeling of mutual understanding and trust.

 In short, you want to approach interviews with a view toward improvement rather than punishment. The best advice is to be a coach, not a judge.

Chapter IX

◆

Coaching

Companies often give a tremendous amount of attention to designing appraisal forms. However, they fail in developing follow-up and coaching programs. Counseling and coaching for improved performance is a most critical element of the evaluation process.

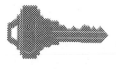 The key to successful coaching is to impress upon employees that you are going to help them attain greater experience and success. You do not want to dwell on the past but concentrate on the future.

Cultivating Employee Strengths

A true executive wants to cultivate the strengths of all employees. Developing strong employees is often done with the knowledge that they may be promoted to other areas of the organization. It's always with mixed emotions when you develop employees to the point where they are promoted to another division or department. By the same token, managers can take great pride in developing persons who go on to much higher levels of responsibility.

I have had a number of bosses in my career and feel that I learned a lot from each one. After leaving a large corporation to start my own company, I am frequently faced with challenging decisions. I often think about how my former bosses would handle a particular situation, and my decisions are often based on the guidance I received from them.

In a large company, employees seek supervisors who have a reputation for developing persons for promotion. Often, the toughest executives are the best at developing people.

Managers can be a coach and not a judge by asking, "What can I do to help you improve your performance?' A smart employee will express appreciation for the offering and respond by requesting greater responsibility and more training.

Improvement Action Plan

During or shortly after the appraisal interview, you want to place in writing plans for improvement. A sample improvement action plan form is shown on the next page.

Progress Report

Many managers find it helpful to complete a progress report following a coaching session. A written record is especially valuable when you have many employees. A sample progress report form is shown on page 100.

Improvement Action Plan

Employee: _____ Date: _____

Performance Improvement Plan from 6–1 to 9–1

Areas in Need of Improvement (in order of importance)	Resources or Assistance Required	Method for Accomplishment	Scheduled Completion Date
1 Improving accuracy of sales forecasting	New computer software	Seek more input from sales force	Ongoing project to be reviewed in 60 days
2 Provide improved sales forecasting to production scheduling	Need additional analyst	New person to be hired	60 days
3 Provide more information for product development	Focus groups to be scheduled every 30 days	No. of focus groups to be increased by contracting with outside research firms	90 days
4			

Employee Progress Report

Name _____ Date_____

Position
Classification _____ Department _____

How long has the person been under your supervision? _____

How well does the employee know the job?

_____

_____

How could job knowledge be improved?

_____

_____

How well is the employee performing in the position in terms of quantity and quality?

_____

_____

How could job performance be improved?

_____

_____

What progress has taken place since the last appraisal?

_____

_____

What specific recommendations have you made for improvement and in what time period?

_____

_____

Signed _____ Date_____

Status Quo Employees

Some employees are content with their present status and are not eager to improve their performance or gain more responsibility. You must recognize that many persons do not want to travel extensively or put in extra hours.

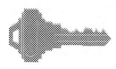 In dealing with status quo employees, you want to evaluate and be guided by the job descriptions. Employees are expected to fulfill their job responsibilities; personal considerations are secondary. However, competent managers will recognize individual situations such as a person who is caring for an ailing parent and if necessary make a strong effort to transfer the employee to a more suitable job in view of the circumstances. A strong manager displays empathy and demonstrates a sincere understanding of employee problems.

 Coaching an outstanding employee is relatively easy and involves considerations such as the following:

1. What type of training would further benefit the employee?

2. Is the employee presently qualified for advancement?

3. When will the employee be qualified for advancement?

4. What higher position or type of position would be suitable for this person?

The Problem Employee

Nearly ever manager will sooner or later face the challenge of handling a problem employee. A competent manager will let the employee know exactly what is unsatisfactory and the improvement measures that will be needed. It is important that the manager not take over the employee's problem. The manager will make every effort to develop and assist in a solution but it is the employee's responsibility to achieve acceptable performance.

A problem employee presents a real coaching challenge. You have several options when coaching a problem employee. Specific considerations are as follows:

1. Make every effort to improve performance to an acceptable level.

2. Recommend a transfer to another department or position where the employee's skills and interests may be better utilized.

3. Initiate a demotion.

4. Recommend termination.

Clearly, option number one aimed at improving performance is the preferred approach. In handling a problem employee, managers need to determine:

1. Why is the performance not satisfactory?

2. What measures can be taken to improve performance?

3. What is a reasonable action and timetable for improvement?

Handling a serious employee problem was much easier several decades ago. If performance was unacceptable, the employee was immediately terminated without much fear of any reprisal. Today, terminations in large corporations usually require a review of the situation by several executives including the supervisor's boss, a HR representative and in some cases, legal counsel.

A problem employee can provide a real challenge to a manager. Improving performance to an acceptable level can be gratifying and clearly in the best interests of the company.

Helpful Words for Coaching and Appraisal Discussions

Following are some helpful words to assist you in your coaching and appraisal discussions:

Accomplish
  achieve
  complete
  carry out
  execute
  fulfill
  make
  perform
Action
  behavior
  conduct
  demeanor
Advise
  caution
  counsel
  instruct
  recommend
  suggest
  warn
Appropriate
  correct
  proper
  suitable
Approval
  favorable
  consent
  sanction
  endorse
Aspiration
  desire
  ambition
  seek

Attribute
  quality
  characteristic
Average
  usual
  normal
Aversion
  dislike
  repugnance
  disgust
Behavior
  conduct
  decorum
  demeanor
  manner
  poise
Capable
  able
  adaptable
  notable
  qualified
  suitable
Closing
  complete
  conclude
  terminate
  to cease
  to end
Commend
  entrust
  praise
  support

Commit
   accountable
   obligation
   pledge
   promise
Competent
   ability
   able
   capable
   proficient
   qualified
   skillful
Concentrate
   attend to
   focus
   ponder
   think
Conduct
   act
   charge
   control
   execute
Confidence
   assurance
   faith
   trust
Consistently
   continuously
   constantly
   faithfully
   frequently
Counsel
   advise
   consult
   guide
Critique
   analyze
   comment
   critique
   review

Decide
   conclude
   determine
   resolve
Decrease
   decline
   diminish
   dwindle
   lower
   reduce
   slack
Demonstrate
   convince
   persuade
   show
Determine
   conclude
   decide
   establish
Develop
   advance
   enlarge
   promote
   difficult
   complex
   hard
   laborious
   puzzling
   strenuous
Discuss
   consider
   converse
   explain
   review
   talk
Distinguish
   identify
   label
   notice
   recognize

Distract
  divert
  draw away
  turn away
Drive
  effort
  effective
  competent
  potent
  practical
Effective
  competent
  potent
  practical
Effort
  apply
  strive
  struggle
  venture
Encourage
  aid
  assure
  exhilarate
Enforce
  force
  compel
  commit
Ensure
  assure
  guarantee
  insure
Exceed
  beat
  better
  outdo
  excel
Excellent
  formulate
  systematic
  express

  plan
Experience
  knowledge
  maturity
  skill
Explore
  search
  examine
  investigate
Express
  make known
  reveal
  show
Extravagant
  excessive
  costly
  wasteful
Fair
  just
  impartial
  unbiased
  objective
Firm
  hard
  solid
  stiff
Flourish
  to blossom
  to grow
  succeed
Focus
  attention
  concentrate
  define
Frank
  candid
  open
  truthful
Frequent
  constant

habitual
Frustrate
    baffle
    balk
Fundamental
    basic
    essential
Good
    suitable
    valid
    genuine
    desirable
Grow
    thrive
    develop
    increase
    cultivate
Guide
    lead
    steer
    help
    aid
    assist
Help
    aid
    assist
Honest
    respect
    honorable
    credible
    commendable
    truthful
    straightforward
Identify
    recognize
    show
    connect
    associate
Implement

enable
make possible
productive means
set up
Imply
    implicit
    understood
    unsaid
    unspoken
Important
    consequential
    considerable
    critical
    essential
    primary
    prominent
    significant
Improve
    better
    more applicable
    more appropriate
    more suitable
    rectify
    upgrade
Inability
    disability
    impotence
    inadequacy
    incompetence
    ineffectiveness
    weakness
Increase
    enlarge
    extend
    greater
    multiply
    raise
Indicate
    gesture

sign
signal
Influence
  convince
  inspire
  persuade
Inform
  advise
  familiarize
  instruct
  teach
  warn
Initiative
  energetic
  enthusiasm
  self-starter
Inspire
  affect
  bring about
  motivate
Insure
  guarantee
  secure
Interest
  attention
  curiosity
  engrossment
Involve
  connect
  comprise
  embrace
  include
Knowledge
  comprehension
  information
  learning
  understanding
  wisdom
Late

behind
belated
tardy
Learn
  discover
  master
  peruse
  study
Maintain
  keep up
  sustain
Manage
  accomplish
  achieve
  command
  conduct
  control
  direct
  guide
  handle
  regulate
Mature
  complete
  develop
  grow
Motivate
  activate
  arouse
  inspire
  prompt
  stimulate
Necessary
  essential
  key
  necessity
  requirement
Negative
  adverse
  unfavorable

Participate
 aid
 cooperate
Perform
 achieve
 accomplish
 act
Persuade
 coax
 convince
 influence
Poor
 deficient
 incomplete
 insufficient
 lacking
 meager
 unfavorable
Positive
 certain
 inevitable
 undeniable
 unquestionable
Possible
 achievable
 attainable
 feasible
 plausible
Potential
 able
 capable
Practice
 drill
 rehearse
 repeat
Praise
 admire
 approve
 command

 compliment
Problem
 difficulty
 dilemma
 issue
 obstacle
 predicament
Proper
 appropriate
 connect
 suitable
Provide
 contribute
 grant
 prepare
 ready
Purpose
 direction
 expectation
 intent
Receive
 accept
 acquire
 obtain
Recognize
 acknowledge
 endorse
Recommend
 advise
 commend
 counsel
 suggest
 urge
Reflect
 deliberate
 mirror
 ponder
Reinforce
 brace

strengthen
support
Require
  demand
  necessitate
  need
  obligate
  order
Respect
  admire
  approve
  esteem
  regard
Response
  answer
  reply
Satisfactory
  adequate
  allowable
  permissible
  sufficient
Skills
  abilities
  readiness
  talent
Solution
  answer
  explanation
  result
Solve
  answer
  explain
  fix
Standards
  ideals
  ethics
  morals
  principles
Strength

power
soundness
vigor
Success
  achieve
  accomplish
  master
  victor
Supervise
  manage
  oversee
Support
  aid
  assist
  help
Tact
  class
  diplomatic
  regard
  poise
Teach
  educate
  drill
  explain
Timely
  prompt
  punctual
Tolerate
  allow
  indulge
  permit
Trust
  certain
  commit
  expectation
  faith
  hope
Understand
  comprehend

grasp
learn
perceive
Unprepared
not ready
unfinished
Unsatisfactory
inadequate
insufficient
unacceptable
unsuitable
wrong
Weak
deficient
fault
feeble
insubstantial
poor
shortcoming

Chapter X

◆

Upper Management Evaluations

Performance appraisals are in universal use at lower levels of a corporation, but they have not been as common at the top management level. In recent years, mobility among top management has dramatically increased. Reasons for high turnover among top management may be attributed to aggressive stock analysts, growing government regulation, global competition, and more demanding boards of directors.

However, recent indications are that more and more members of top management are being formally appraised. Management evaluators at the highest level will best serve a corporation by concentrating on the following factors:

- Earnings

- Sales

- Vision

- Leadership

- Strategic planning

- Organizing

- Communications
- Management succession

Special considerations are present when evaluating top executives. After all, most executives are inherently ambitious, competent, and high achievers. The normal bell-shaped curve remains in effect among top executives although at a higher level.

Executives need to understand that performance appraisals are a serious management responsibility at all levels and are not just a routine HR matter.

A common tendency is for an executive to believe that periodic reviews become increasingly irrelevant as they progress up the ladder into higher management. Actually, reviews at higher levels become more important because management personnel face greater responsibilities that can have a significant impact on the future of the entire organization.

Performance appraisals are now being conducted in a work environment that places greater emphasis on team skills and committee actions. Executives are being bombarded by an increasing number of influences beyond their control such as legislation, environmental concerns, and global competition.

It is sometimes difficult to evaluate an executive on decision making, for example, when complex decisions are the result of joint efforts of many executives representing different fields of expertise.

Many executives are often egotistical and may have delusions about their true performance. Executives often tend to be unrealistic in their goal setting and expectations. They frequently find it difficult to accept constructive criticism from senior executives.

It must also be recognized that the growing use of employment contracts at high management levels may negate the use of performance appraisals. Provisions in the contract may call for performance and compensation to be based on hard data such as sales increases, higher earnings, and rising stock prices.

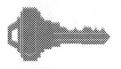 Keep in mind that the higher a person advances in management, the more time should be devoted to managing and controlling and less on operating. Appraisal forms for operational personnel are not suitable for management-level positions.

Top management personnel who are evaluated themselves will view appraisal programs with greater interest and support. Evaluations of top management benefit the entire corporation including shareholders.

Chapter XI

◆

Evaluating Distant Employees

Corporate mergers, global business and telecommunications have greatly changed the workplace for millions of employees. The growth in the number of persons working out of their homes is staggering. Offices with one or several employees are now scattered across the country. Companies are often establishing operations in rural areas. Despite geographic distances, these employees are as close to the home office as never before via modern telecommunications.

Evaluating employees located in foreign countries is especially difficult. Different cultures, customs, languages, laws, and currencies add an entirely new dimension to appraisals. Standard evaluation forms may be totally unsuitable for employees located in foreign countries.

In the absence of direct contact, quantitative factors are about the only means of objective measurement. The need for predetermined standards are essential such as sales, market share, and productivity. Nevertheless, every effort should be made to have at least one face-to-face meeting with distant employees on an annual or semi-annual basis.

Chapter XII

◆

Self-Appraisals

Many companies believe that the use of self-appraisals strengthens the evaluation process. Subordinates often feel that they are required to assume a passive role and merely listen to criticisms and improvement suggestions without having an opportunity to defend themselves. One-sided evaluations can result in loss of morale and destructive attitudes. On the other hand, self-appraisals can generate open communications in the employee-manager relationship.

Companies using self-appraisals distribute them about ten days before the scheduled interview. The employee is told at the same time that the supervisor will also evaluate the person using the identical form. During the interview, the two appraisals may be compared and in some cases a third form may be prepared.

Employees who consistently overrate themselves need to be brought back down to earth using objective facts.

My experience with a very large corporation is that most employees are fairly realistic in appraising themselves. Many employees actually underrate themselves.

Critics of self-appraisals claim that they make the evaluation system too easy for supervisors who are reluctant to face confrontations.

Chapter XIII

◆

360-Degree Appraisals

One of the biggest and most controversial developments in recent years has been the so-called 360-degree performance review. Under this system, your performance is appraised by a circle of persons in your work environment including supervisors, coworkers, subordinates, and even suppliers and customers. In many cases, the reviews are anonymous and the appraised person may or may not share the feedback with supervisors.

The objective of multiple reviews is to provide feedback that will make a person more aware of strengths and weaknesses that can be cultivated for the benefit of the organization.

Key considerations in a 360-degree program are as follows:

- Cooperation
- Open communication
- Sharing information
- Confidentiality
- Meeting deadlines
- Providing back-up support

The danger of 360-degree appraisals is that they can turn a division or department into a social club. Persons who try to please everyone may please no one and lose sight of their basic job function. The fear of negative reviews may influence a manager to become indecisive and to avoid taking risks and forceful action. Moreover, multiple ratings can cause alienation and affect morale.

Since a basic tenet of an appraisal system is to evaluate performance against a pre-existing standard, 360-degree reviews tend to be very subjective rather than objective. The evaluator may have little knowledge of another person's job description. As a result, 360-degree reviews can easily become a congeniality contest.

A 360-degree program is job security for HR personnel. It requires attending seminars, holding orientation sessions and, of course, designing and distributing loads of paper or electronic forms. It is strictly a supplemental training aid and is no substitute for a sound appraisal program used for development and compensation purposes.

Chapter XIV

◆

Multiple Supervisors

Downsizing in many organizations has frequently resulted in persons working for more than one supervisor. Secretaries were once assigned mainly to one executive. Today, secretaries may report to several executives, each competing for equal time and often creating a highly political environment.

Nevertheless, persons working for several executives have a primary and formal relationship to one individual, usually a senior executive. The manager with an employee who also works for other persons must be extremely tactful in completing an appraisal form. In such cases, the primary supervisor must be extremely objective in appraising performance and recognize the inherent difficulties and conflicting forces competing for the employee's services.

 The senior executive must understand that a direct subordinate also working for others will give priority to the primary boss, often causing resentment and conflict. The comments of others may be highly subjective and must be viewed with caution.

Chapter XV

◆

Employee Surveys

Employee Satisfaction Surveys

Performance appraisals in some companies are being supplemented by employee satisfaction surveys. These surveys are often done periodically and employees are sometimes selected at random. Surveys may focus on job satisfaction or even on an employee's view of their immediate supervisor.

Questions on employee satisfaction surveys sometimes ask the employee to rate the boss on such factors as feedback, support, and fairness in evaluating employees. Questions frequently focus on the following:

Does your supervisor maintain open communication?

Does your supervisor provide satisfactory feedback?

Does your supervisor provide needed support?

Does your supervisor fairly evaluate performance?

Does your supervisor welcome suggestions and ideas?

Many executives believe that employee satisfaction is a key management responsibility and should be considered along with performance appraisals when establishing compensation and bonuses.

Companies often take pride in rewarding executives who are well-liked by their employees. On the other hand, critics of employee surveys take the position that business is not a personality contest and that management personnel should concentrate on meeting Wall Street expectations.

Satisfaction surveys can be unreliable because many employees, regardless of management assurances, are fearful of criticizing their immediate supervisor. These surveys can quickly become a "congeniality contest" and actually exert a negative influence on a company's performance. Employee surveys especially for compensation purposes are clearly no substitute for a sound appraisal program.

Management Audits

Sometimes management audits are conducted because of changes in ownership, technology, or market conditions. A new CEO may wish to learn of the strengths and weaknesses of everyone in the organization.

Many companies delegate personnel audits to a senior executive. The advantage of an in-house audit is that the executive has an intimate knowledge of the organization.

However, there are a number of disadvantages of an in-house audit. The objectivity of a senior executive may be questionable, especially when the person may have responsibility for poor performers. The judgment of a senior executive may also be clouded even subconsciously by personal friendships.

A strong case exists for having an outside consultant conduct a special audit of HR. The outside person is likely to be more objective and experienced. Moreover, the final report from an outside consultant (obviously an out-of-town expert) is likely to be better accepted by others in senior management, as well as by the board of directors and shareholders.

Chapter XVI

◆

Legal Considerations

HR executives tend to emphasize the development aspects of performance reviews. However, appraisals also are needed to protect the company from lawsuits. Employers at one time had to be largely concerned with federal protective benefits not covered by state legislation. Today, however, states and even some cities are increasingly enacting employment legislation. Several years ago, a bill was even introduced in the Ohio Legislature that would provide executives immunity from lawsuits if they believed that the statements in a performance evaluation were truthful and restricted to actual work performance.

The entire HR function is now being highly influenced by legal and governmental considerations. Carelessness in administering HR programs may result in your company being targeted by a government agency. Many companies are being advised to not even disclose performance information on job reference requests.

Following are two examples of the critical need for accuracy in appraisals.

1. Too Little, Too Late

Let's assume one of your employees has a poor attendance record, has failed to meet deadlines, and is seriously impairing the performance of your department. You simply want to terminate the employee.

You go to your HR department to discuss termination procedures. The very first response of the HR representative is to review the most recent performance evaluation.

"Why did you give this person a relatively high rating just two months ago?" The representative asks. You respond that the employee is very sensitive and is not able to accept constructive criticism. Moreover, you point out that the person has encountered some financial problems and your compassion influenced you to make sure that a reasonable pay increase would be granted.

The HR person asks what documentation you may have concerning the problem employee. You respond that you previously had some discussions with the employee but that nothing was ever placed in writing and signed by the employee.

At this point, the HR representative says that termination is not possible at this time because of the favorable review that is a matter of company record.

2. Document, Document, Document

Now, assume that you have a similar situation with an employee who is seriously under performing. You go to the HR department to discuss termination procedures. The HR representative immediately opens the file and brings out your last review of the employee. The review shows that you

have given the employee an unacceptable rating in every category and that the employee signed the appraisal.

Next, you present a series of documented reports. You provide a report showing the exact number of absences during the past six months, which is signed by the employee. Then, you show a policy on absenteeism from the employee handbook. You also produce a report showing that the company failed to receive a large order because the bid was submitted after a deadline. Finally, you hand over a document signed by you, an observer, and the employee outlining a warning discussion on a specific date at a specific time stating that termination would be forthcoming if the employee fails to meet the measurement standards covered in the job description.

With factual information of this type, HR will take action. The three most important words in real estate may be *location, location, location* but in termination situations the three most important words are *documentation, documentation, documentation.* In a discriminatory lawsuit, the plaintiff's attorney in the discovery process will promptly issue a subpoena for personnel records with the evaluation form being a prime target.

Performance appraisals in previous decades were very general and subjective. Rating forms included factors such as appearance and personality. Today's litigious work environment has forced the need for more valid and objective standards of measurement.

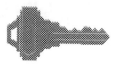 You want to avoid any reference on an appraisal form or in an interview to age, race, religion, gender, marital status, child care, politics, smoking, and other sensitive areas.

In the case of an unlawful discharge lawsuit, there is always the possibility that a claim will be made of negligent evaluation. Damages have been awarded to employees on the assertion that periodic evaluations were not performed with reasonable care and that the appraisal process gave no indication that dismissal was imminent.

In many respects, the U.S. Congress is now running the HR department of the nation's organizations. Today, you cannot read a HR publication without seeing articles on government agencies or employment law.

Raters cannot be expected to keep informed of all legislation affecting the workplace. HR people have a great responsibility to properly train and keep evaluators informed of legal concerns involving the workplace, especially with appraisals.

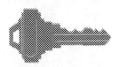 Accuracy and honesty in documenting employee performance is a priority of the highest order.

Chapter XVII

◆

Downfalls of Appraisals

After a new appraisal program is introduced and the whistles, sirens, and balloons are over, a system can quickly degenerate. A strong program requires on-going attention in an organization with sound HR policies.

Many managers dread appraisal time. They simply feel that they know how well a person is performing and that there is no need for a formal program.

Some managers find it extremely difficult to sit down face-to-face with an employee and review performance. It's far easier to conduct an interview with an outstanding employee than with one who needs serious improvement.

Weak managers may downplay the importance of appraisals by making them appear to be trivial. For example, consider the following one-sided conversation:

Supervisor:
> "Hey Joe, got a minute? I just got a form from my boss concerning your performance. I just filled it out and thought you would want to see it. I know it's no big deal because you're doing a good job. Take a couple of

minutes to look it over, sign here, and I'll get this thing off my desk."

The foregoing manager is simply not fulfilling the responsibilities of a supervisory position. It is clearly a "cop-out" and is not in the best interest of the employee or employer.

A manager who is very uncomfortable with performance reviews must recognize that the responsibility goes with the territory and that the manager is being paid to be a manager.

Consistency and accuracy in ratings may also be adversely affected by employment conditions. A few years ago, low ratings would have been given to employees with frequent absences, tardiness, or even for insubordination. In a tight labor market, offenses that would have once resulted in a dismissal may be treated as inconveniences.

Employee misconduct is being given an unprecedented degree of leniency. The high cost of recruiting, training, and retaining skilled workers may easily influence an evaluator to give higher but unjustified ratings. Managers simply want to ensure bigger pay increases to keep employees from leaving. Once a labor market softens, evaluators may return to more stringent ratings.

As a result, a long-term employee's rating chart may resemble a roller coaster despite a consistent level of performance. "Rating inflation" can easily weaken an otherwise sound appraisal program.

The increasing job mobility in organizational life can have a strong impact on appraisal programs. A manager who is about to retire or leave the company often has a tendency to reward loyal employees with very high ratings. The incoming manager will thereby inherit a delicate situation where concurrence may be lacking. In a large organization, a high rate of turnover among managers may destroy the consistency of evaluations and create problems with employee morale.

Problems arise when persons receive unwarranted high ratings and remain with an organization for many years. The job market may change but appraisal records are permanent and are difficult to lower in such cases.

Every large organization has managers who consistently rate high. Managers may give high ratings for self-serving reasons. They wish to make an impression with superiors that they have the strong ability to develop people as evidenced by the high ratings assigned to their employees.

Inflated ratings can penalize employees when decisions are made concerning promotions and transfers. A manager who develops a reputation for high ratings may actually be doing a disservice to career-oriented employees. Regardless of how management may view rater tendencies, the fact remains that completed forms are a matter of company record.

When faced with a long period of inflated ratings, companies sometimes introduce an entirely new evaluation program. The purpose is to provide a fresh start and bring ratings back down to a realistic level. Employees can recognize the true reason for a new system and often experience greater anxiety and disenchantment.

Some executives believe that a formal appraisal program is a waste of time, money, and energy. They take the position, "I know how all of my employees are performing—that's why I am paid to be an executive. If anyone is not performing up to my expectations, I will remove them."

Another basic problem is that standard appraisal forms are often used to evaluate all employees regardless of job duties. "Dealing with the public" is certainly appropriate for customer service personnel but not for an internal bookkeeper.

Performance appraisals are often viewed as a self-serving program to keep HR staff people busy. Too often, the newly revised appraisal form with the transmittal memo is seen as an end in itself. Annual or semi-annual evaluations can easily become a mechanical ritual with harried managers viewing them as an unnecessary burden to be quickly completed and disposed of.

Some HR people recognize the value of appraisals but dread the blizzard of paperwork and computer programming that are associated with them. They also feel that it is impossible to please everyone and appraisals often create undesirable resentment, especially in times of a tight labor market.

Performance appraisal systems often suffer from the increasing mobility of HR personnel. A company may have an excellent and time-proven evaluation program for many years. Once a new director of HR arrives, you can usually be sure that a new appraisal program will soon follow.

The new executive wants to impress higher management, and obviously a new appraisal program will be needed to achieve the organization's new goals.

 Problems arise when appraisal systems are changed frequently because the continuity for long-term employees becomes questionable. You want to revise evaluations only when required to maintain accuracy or to meet organizational changes.

Avoiding Negative Influences

 Despite the best planning and management, there are a number of factors that can negatively influence the success of an appraisal program. By recognizing negative influences, managers can take steps to avoid them. Factors that can undermine evaluation programs are as follows:

1. Lack of top management support
2. Lead time for completion is too short
3. Managers have too many direct subordinates, making honest appraisals difficult
4. Managers have little control over compensation and believe the appraisal system is irrelevant
5. Persons are promoted by upper management with little consideration given to evaluation and assessment programs
6. Promotions are based on non-performance factors such as nepotism, golfing skills, and social considerations
7. Promotions are based on academic backgrounds rather than on job performance
8. Key positions are frequently filled by outsiders
9. Managers are required to complete too many lengthy evaluation and follow-up forms

Other factors that can negatively influence appraisals are:

Critical Incidents
Some managers may allow a single incident that may have occurred months ago to influence ratings

Recent Incidents
Managers may evaluate on the basis of a few recent examples of performance rather than a broader view across time

Senior Employees
A manager's performance ratings my be significantly influenced by an employee who has an exten-

sive length of service. Younger managers frequently find it especially difficult to evaluate senior employees who have been involved with appraisals for decades.

Previous Ratings

Sometimes managers are reluctant to realistically evaluate a person because previous supervisors have given the person very high ratings. Executives who are about to retire frequently give a long and dedicated employee an exceptionally high rating in appreciation for many years of loyal service.

Experienced managers know that only a select few will receive a maximum pay increase. A manager may have an average employee who is experiencing serious health problems. Another employee may be encountering financial problems because of personal difficulties. When confronted with such situations, any reasonable manager would feel compassionate. Problems arise when programs are undermined whenever sympathy and non-performance considerations enter into the evaluation process and employees are given inflated ratings for compensation purposes.

Sometimes, companies elect to reward all employees following a financial windfall. A company may experience unusually large annual or quarterly profits. If an identical bonus, for example, is given to each employee, the poor performers benefit equally with the high performers. An employee may quickly recognize that management is not guided by performance ratings, and the entire evaluation program is irrelevant.

As mentioned earlier, many employees believe the true evaluation of their performance is reflected in the paycheck. In a "pay for performance program," a one-time special compensation equally distributed to all employees can weaken an appraisal system.

Another employment policy that can negatively affect performance appraisals is a tendency to fill key positions from outside the company. A firm that emphasizes the improvement objectives of evaluations must make every effort to promote from within. Employees who are passed over for promotions that are filled by outsiders quickly turn negative on evaluations, causing serious morale problems.

One of the most serious downfalls affecting appraisal systems is the offering of special inducements to attract highly skilled workers who are in strong demand. Companies may offer compensation and benefit programs to prospective workers that far exceed those of existing employees. Long-term employees who have spent many hours in appraisal sessions can be devastated upon learning of greater benefits and higher pay extended to a new recruit who may have also received a signing bonus.

A new person will frequently assume that all employees in similar positions have identical benefits and speak freely. Moreover, the Internet now allows employees to research salary information in their industry. As a result of compensation discrepancies, distrust of the appraisal program can become widespread, resulting in serious morale problems throughout the organization.

In evaluating upper management personnel, special benefits given to select employees can seriously weaken a formal evaluation program. Frequently, a recruit for a key position will be able to negotiate a company car, greater stock options, and perhaps a club membership. Although compensation and stock options among lower-level executives can be kept confidential, more obvious symbols such as a large office, a company car, privileged parking, and club memberships fast become common knowledge. Long-term employees in similar positions without equal benefits will look upon appraisals as a system that is easily ignored by top management.

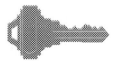 A sound evaluation program can only function in an open environment where benefits are provided on clearly defined levels of responsibility.

Managers need to also be aware of efforts by employees to exert a positive influence on appraisals. For example, an employee may have an idea for a new production method or an idea that will please the boss and higher management. If the person knows that evaluations will take place in October, there will be a strong tendency to present the idea in September so that it will be a timely and positive topic during the October appraisal. After all, how is a boss going to be overly critical after an employee has just made the supervisor look good to upper management. Employees may also tend to work longer hours and exhibit strong creativity and enthusiasm shortly before appraisal time.

 You always want to be careful about making any casual comments about a person's performance. For example, assume that an employee is enjoying a once-a-year golf outing with the boss. After a long summer day, imagine the following conversation taking place in the parking lot.

Employee:
      "If you were completing my performance appraisal today, how would you say I am doing?"

Supervisor:
      "You're doing great. Keep up the good work."

The next morning, the employee types out a memo for the record, confirming the boss's comments.

Now consider this conversation between the two several months later in a formal appraisal interview:

Supervisor:
      "You have some problems that definitely need improvement."

Employee:
"I what? Why you just told me a couple of months ago that I was doing great. In fact, here's a memo to myself recording your comments. I don't understand."

The foregoing situation puts the supervisor on the defensive and is clearly self-inflicted.

No one can be criticized for asking the boss for performance feedback. In fact, some management experts recommend the practice in order to avoid compounding problems. Managers must carefully consider performance comments to ensure accuracy and consistency.

The economic impact of performance appraisals now extends far beyond pay increases. For most of the Twentieth Century, pensions were considered to be a sacred benefit provided by the employer. Employees were rewarded for long-term employment with financial security during their retirement years.

With today's younger workers unlikely to spend a career with one company, the traditional pension plan is fast fading. Personal investment programs and stock options are becoming the retirement programs of the new economy. As a result, responsibility for the retirement years is shifting from the employer to the employee.

Employees in many corporations have become strong participants in a variety of company-sponsored investment programs. Employer contributions to a profit sharing plan, for example, are directly related to the employee's compensation.

Stock options are another important area of great interest to many employees. Fortunes can be made in a rapidly rising stock market. Clearly, performance appraisal ratings may have a tremendous impact on a person's economic well-being. A danger exists that the economic implications of ratings may be gradually overshadowing the incentive for improvement in itself.

Impact of Technology

The enormous benefits of technology are often exerting a strong impact on measuring individual performance. The information explosion is making interdependence among managers more critical within the organization. If a person's effectiveness is dependent on the efforts of other departments, it is becoming difficult in many situations to evaluate individual performance.

Computerization is profoundly affecting the workplace. In the retail area, for example, cash registers at large chains are transmitting inventory information with lightning fast speed to home office computers. Inventories and demand are now being tracked by the minute.

In addition to the direct data from the stores, home office computers are receiving information from a number of individuals and departments. Computers are processing data coming in from all over the world such as the number of new store openings, style changes, seasonal demand, climate changes, currency fluctuations, labor rates, environmental concerns, taxes etc. Individual contributions in such situations are frequently becoming more difficult to accurately measure.

As another example, should field sales personnel receive credit for purchases made over the Internet? A field sales person may generate strong advertising and promotional support at the local level. However, determining whether the Internet purchase was influenced by field work or by an attractive web site is difficult.

In many respects, technology is shifting responsibilities to more of a team effort. A group of managers working together to benefit the entire organization may be more critical than one individual's performance. The present day world of fast communications and networks of systems is producing a tremendous amount of information. While individual contributions in some situations may be diminishing, higher management must accept overall responsibility and is clearly subject to evaluation.

 Finally and perhaps the most common problem in the appraisal process is to give too little attention to improvement. It's a simple matter to merely check some boxes, but it takes some thought to determine how and why specific skills need to be improved. Companies often design a form and distribute copies to all supervisors and believe that they have an effective evaluation system in place. Nothing could be further from the truth. Improving performance is the ultimate goal.

Summary of Key Points

(to be reviewed prior to each rating period)

Chapter I: Trends and Developments

1. Recognize the current objectives of performance appraisals:

    a. To identify the strengths and weaknesses of employees

    b. To identify the growth potential of employees

    c. To provide information for employee development

    d. To make the organization more productive

    e. To provide data for the fair compensation of employees

    f. To protect the organization from unlawful discharge lawsuits

2. Use appraisals as a recruiting tool.

3. Seek essential top management support of appraisal programs.

Chapter II: Defining Job Descriptions

1. Prepare a job analysis including the degree of experience, skills, and ability required for each position.
2. Prepare a job description for every position outlining basic responsibilities, duties, and measurements of performance.
3. Monitor and continuously update job descriptions and salary classifications.

Chapter III: What to Evaluate

1. Use both quantitative and qualitative rating factors.
2. Select performance rating characteristics based on relevancy to the position.

Chapter IV: When to Evaluate

1. Rate everyone at the same time.
2. Rate newer employees at shorter intervals.

Chapter V: Designing the Form

1. Keep appraisal forms concise and simple, preferably no more than three pages.
2. Include rating instructions on the appraisal form.
3. Allow space for comments and overall appraisal.
4. Include space for both the supervisor's and the employee's signatures and dates.
5. Print the form on high-quality paper.
6. Monitor forms continuously but only revise to maintain accuracy.
7. Keep appraisals confidential.

Chapter VI: How to Rate

1. Remember that the common objective is to mutually improve performance.

2. Evaluate persons on what has taken place, not on the promise of future performance.

3. Confine ratings to the period since the last appraisal.

4. Rate on the basis of previously established performance standards and not in comparison with others.

5. Do not confuse activity with accomplishment.

6. Rate performance and not personality.

7. Remember the bell-shaped curve.

8. Do not allow your personality to influence ratings.

9. Complete appraisals in draft form for later review and completion.

10. Complete appraisals at a quiet setting removed from your workplace.

11. Use the sandwich approach in constructive criticism by first mentioning strengths, then areas in need of improvement, followed by compliments.

12. Complete appraisals promptly.

13. Remind yourself prior to rating that you have a moral and legal obligation to be fair and objective.

14. Do not rate a person good or poorly on all factors based on a single experience or incident.

15. Avoid inflated ratings and rate on true measures of performance.

16. Do not be unusually critical or over demanding with any individual.

17. Do not rate everyone as average regardless of performance.

18. Consider factors outside the control of employees.

19. Ensure that all evaluators are properly trained.

Chapter VII: Scoring

1. Rank all employees by general classifications of positions such as management, administrative, clerical, technical, and sales.

2. Use common sense relative to the position in assigning values to characteristics such as accuracy.

Chapter VIII: The Interview

1. Recognize that the rating form is only one element of the evaluation process.

2. Handle problems as they occur and do not save them for discussion in the appraisal interview.

3. Maintain open communication by keeping employees informed of their performance to avoid anxiety and surprises in the interview.

4. Prepare thoroughly for the interview by anticipating objectives and problems.

5. Bring important documents to the interview for possible back-up use.

6. Schedule the interview about ten days in advance, preferably early in the week.

7. Conduct the interview in a neutral setting such as a conference room.

8. Consider sitting side-by-side with the employee during the interview.

9. Ask the employee, "In what ways do you feel you could improve yourself?"

10. Keep in mind the three key words in interviews: honesty, openness, and trust.

11. Listen and do not dominate the interview.

12. Keep the interview job-related.

13. Do not use the interview to discuss compensation, fringe benefits, or promotion.

14. Avoid negative words such as *failure, unsatisfactory,* or *problem areas* unless absolutely necessary.

15. Do not discuss performance in general terms but be as specific as possible.

16. Focus on future solutions and improvements.

17. Establish improvement areas and timetables, especially for problem employees.

18. Record all action plans in writing either in the appraisal form or in a separate communication.

19. Use positive reinforcement at every opportunity.

20. Make every effort to build morale.

21. Impress upon employees that evaluation is a continuous program.

22. End the interview on a note of mutual understanding and trust.

23. Be a coach, not a judge.

Chapter IX: Coaching

1. Concentrate on cultivating the strengths of employees.

2. Impress upon employees that you want to help them achieve greater responsibilities and success.

3. Make sure that "status quo" employees understand that they are being evaluated on the measurement standards

outlined in the job description, regardless of their personal career aspirations.

Chapter X: Upper Management Evaluations

1. Encourage performance evaluations of upper management using broad based goals and objective measurement standards.

Chapter XI: Evaluating Distant Employees

1. Develop highly objective and quantitative standards for distant employees.

2. Plan at least one annual face-to-face meeting with distant employees.

Chapter XII: Self-Appraisals

1. Distribute self-appraisals using the identical form about ten days before the scheduled interview.

Chapter XIII: 360-Degree Appraisals

1. Recognize that 360-degree appraisals can easily turn into a congeniality contest with undesirable results.

2. Use 360-degree appraisals as a training aid and not for evaluation purposes.

Chapter XIV: Multiple Supervisors

1. Recognize that employees working for multiple supervisors face conflicting demands that must be carefully considered.

Chapter XV: Employee Surveys

1. Do not use employee surveys as a substitute for a formal evaluation program.

Chapter XVI: Legal Considerations

1. Ensure that your ratings are honest and objective and based on facts and pre-established standards.
2. Use factual documentation at every opportunity, especially with problem employees.
3. Avoid all references to age, gender, race, and other sensitive areas.

Chapter XVII: Downfalls of Appraisals

1. Do not downplay the importance of appraisals.
2. Avoid inflated ratings.
3. Be aware of negative factors that can influence ratings.
4. Avoid viewing appraisals as an end in themselves rather than as an ongoing improvement program.

About the Author

James E. Neal Jr. holds a B.B.A. degree from the University of Toledo and a M.A. degree from the Institute of Labor and Industrial Relations of the University of Illinois. He has served in management human resources positions with a major international corporation. He founded Neal Publications, Inc. in 1978 and is the author of five books including the best-selling *Effective Phrases for Performance Appraisals* now in its ninth edition with 57 total printings.

Index

Notes

Notes

Notes

Notes

Notes

Notes